The Ultimate Guide to Differentiation

OTHER TITLES BY SUE COWLEY

How to Survive Your First Year in Teaching, Third Edition

Getting the Buggers to Behave, Fifth Edition

Getting the Buggers to Write, Third Edition

Getting the Buggers to Think, Second Edition

Getting the Buggers into Drama

Getting Your Little Darlings to Behave

Guerilla Guide to Teaching: The Definitive Resource for New Teachers, Second Edition

The Ultimate Guide to Differentiation

Achieving excellence for all

Sue Cowley

BLOOMSBURY
LONDON • OXFORD • NEW YORK • NEW DELHI • SYDNEY

Bloomsbury Education
An imprint of Bloomsbury Publishing Plc

50 Bedford Square, London, WC1B 3DP, UK
1385 Broadway, New York, NY 10018, USA
29 Earlsfort Terrace, Dublin 2, Ireland

www.bloomsbury.com

First published 2018

A catalogue record for this book is available from the British Library.

ISBN PB: 978-1-4729-4896-0
ePub: 978-1-4729-4894-6
ePDF: 978-1-4729-4895-3

8 10 9 7

Typeset by Newgen KnowledgeWorks Pvt. Ltd., Chennai, India
Printed and bound in Great Britain by CPI Group (UK) Ltd, Croydon CR0 4YY

Contents

Acknowledgements

Thanks to Di Leedham for her insights and advice about differentiating for learners with EAL and for allowing me to share her ideas in this book. Thanks to Nancy Gedge and Jules Daulby for their wisdom about all things SEND-related and for letting me use their suggestions here. Thank you to the team at Bloomsbury for making this book a reality. And thanks and love as always to my family for making it possible for me to be a writer.

Introduction

In the very simplest terms, differentiation is about using different approaches with our learners, so that they can all make the maximum progress in their learning. It is about accepting that the learners we work with are all different – that they know, understand and can do different things at the point when we come to teach them. While it is not necessarily easy to differentiate, particularly for a class that you do not see very often, it is part and parcel of a philosophy of inclusive education. We tend to think of differentiation as something very obvious and time-consuming – preparing a variety of worksheets for different learners, for instance. But in reality, it is the subtle, flexible and responsive approaches you use that are the nuts and bolts of everyday differentiation, rather than the specific techniques that you might be able to spell out in a lesson plan. In essence, reacting to each learner's individual needs is what 'good teaching' looks like, because it allows every individual to learn. Differentiation is an attempt to start from where individual learners are at any given moment, and to move them forward from that point.

In this book I will show you that differentiation does not have to be about a big, grand, complicated set of approaches requiring the application of lots of time and money; it is more about all the practical adaptations that good teachers make, day in, day out. As an educator you react differently to different learners because you know that they need different things. For learners who need a lot of support to learn, for instance those with SEND (special educational needs and disabilities), differentiation can be vital for helping them to access the curriculum. For learners who are already way ahead of what the curriculum asks of them, differentiation is important for pushing them and keeping them challenged and engaged. This book outlines a host of practical ways in which you can support, stretch and challenge all your learners, whatever their needs.

Every class is made up of a collection of individuals, and each learner within the class will have had a different set of experiences, before the point at which you begin to teach them. These experiences will not just be about what has happened to them in school, they will also (and often mainly) be about what has happened to them outside of it, because children and young people spend a lot more time not in school than in it. Your learners will have different kinds of interests in and aptitudes for various subjects and they will have varied home, social and cultural backgrounds as well. Your learners will have diverse levels and types of knowledge and they will have picked up different amounts and types of vocabulary. Some of your learners may have travelled the world, while others may never have left the area where they were born. Your learners will have distinct and unique personalities as well. Even if differentiation wasn't a key part of the expected standards for qualified teachers, it seems obvious that we would want to differentiate to try to meet the varying needs of any group of people.

Differentiation is as much about an attitude to children and young people as it is about an attitude to teaching. If we see 'the class' as a single entity, and plan with that in mind, the learning will only be at the right level for a handful of learners – it is likely to be too easy for some, and too hard for others. This mismatch between what we are teaching and what our learners are learning means that they cannot make as much progress as might otherwise be possible. Each and every individual that we teach will have their own strengths, and indeed weaknesses, but these may lie in very different areas. By embracing the need to differentiate, we celebrate the diversity of the learners in our care. We see difference as something to be appreciated and enjoyed – something that adds to the rich tapestry of the classroom – rather than as something that can only ever add to our workload and slow us down in our teaching.

Taking the need for differentiation on board requires us to start from the viewpoint of the individual, rather than from the viewpoint of the teacher. Just because we teach something to the whole class, that does not mean that everyone in the class will have learnt it. We need to see our goal as ensuring that everyone has *learnt* x, y or z, rather than ensuring that we have *taught* it. And this means taking the learners' differences into account in the way that we plan for and teach them. For instance, while one learner in your class might know everything there is to know about dinosaurs, and may have memorised hundreds of their names, another learner might have experienced life in three different countries, and be fluent in several languages. While one learner in your class might struggle with retaining times tables, another might have difficulty in using full stops. While one might be great at listening and focusing, another might find it desperately hard to sit still. In a mixed age group in a small primary school, where the teacher might have three different year groups in a single class, differentiation is more than just a model of good practice – it is an absolute necessity.

In order to differentiate effectively, we need to figure out what the individual currently knows or can do, and then work out what that learner needs to know or learn how to do next. If we don't manage to do this, some learners might already know what we are teaching them, and others might not be able to access what we are teaching them at all. There is no point in presenting an individual with learning that they find impossible to understand; nor is it a good use of time to teach someone something they already know or can do. As noted previously, to be effective, we need to try to meet each learner at the point they are at now, and move them forwards from that point. However, as every teacher understands, with a class of perhaps 30 or more learners, this is easy to say but remarkably difficult to do. In a secondary school, where a teacher of a 'once a week' subject might see 250 or more learners over the course of a week, it can feel like a task of mammoth proportions. But even if we can't manage to differentiate as fully as we might like, we can still make small tweaks to our practice that will make a big difference to our learners.

Differentiation is a key concern for the teachers that I meet and work with – how can they adapt to the needs of every learner in their classes, yet at the same time stretch and challenge them? How can they show that they are 'doing differentiation', in a way that senior leaders or inspectors will understand? With funding going down, class sizes going up, and teachers expected to get every individual to 'make progress', differentiation is going to become ever more crucial in doing the best for everyone. Senior leaders and inspectors all say that they want to see effective differentiation going on in classrooms, but what exactly does 'effective differentiation' look like? This book will help you to answer that question, so that you feel confident to say 'this is how I am differentiating and this is how it is helping my learners to learn'. Differentiation categorically does not have to be about creating separate worksheets for different groups of learners – it can and should be about a great deal more than that.

One way that schools try to make differentiation a bit easier is by setting their learners, either into different classes, organised as sets or streams, in a secondary school, or into different attainment groupings within a single class at primary. The idea is that this creates a smaller range of difference between the learners, thus making it easier for the teacher to match the teaching and learning to their current attainment. There is a lot of research into the impact that setting or streaming can have on progress, motivation and outcomes for different groups of learners. While it might work well for some groups, it can be highly problematic for your lowest attainers, because of the impact on motivation, self-image and the need for higher-attaining role models. In any case, even if you or your school use attainment groupings rather than teaching mixed-ability groups, there will still be significant differences from one learner to the next within a class.

This book is at once an impassioned defence of the pedagogical necessity of differentiation, and also a practical, realistic and time-saving guide to 'doing differentiation' in real-life classroom situations. The advice in the book is designed to be accessible and easy to dip in and out of for busy teachers on the hunt for tips and strategies. The approaches will work for different age groups, from the youngest children right up to post-compulsory learners. In this book I hope to demonstrate to you that you already differentiate much of the time, in subtle and often creative ways. It is important that we acknowledge and celebrate the variety of approaches that we already use to cater for all our learners – for too long teachers have been quiet about the skills they have in this area. I hope that this book will give you confidence in your own professional judgement, as well as some fresh ideas and ways to develop your skills even further, so that you can meet the challenge to support and stretch every single learner.

Sue Cowley
www.suecowley.co.uk

Chapter 1
Planning

Before you can differentiate effectively in your lessons, you need to get to know more about your learners, so that you can plan and prepare for the kind of differentiation you might need to do for them. It could be that you have to get a specific resource ready to aid some learners; maybe you need to organise a source of support for an individual; perhaps you want to think about groupings, decide what order to present the material in, or think about what questions to ask of which learners. But to a large extent, you will only be able to plan to do these things once you know something about your learners. Until you have an idea of where they are in their learning at the moment, it is very difficult to figure out where they might need to go next. Of course, this presents a dilemma to any educator as they start working with a new group. We have to teach them *something* even if we're not sure whether it is the something that they most need to learn at that moment.

This first part of this book looks at the kinds of pre-planning that can go into differentiation, both before you meet a group for the first time, and as you get to know them. It deals with everything that an educator can do before a lesson, focusing on time-efficient and realistic ways to plan for differentiated learning. The more you get to know a class, the better you will be able to plan and prepare for them. However, even when you know them really well, learners will often surprise you by what they know, what they can do, or what they think and say. Even when you have planned carefully for differentiation, remember to stay flexible, and to stay open to the possibility that your learners might know more (or less) than you had anticipated, or that they might not be able to grasp a concept in the way you are explaining it.

One of the keys to effective differentiation is to be responsive to what is actually going on in front of you. Our learners will often confound us when, instead of the reactions we had expected to get to a particular piece of learning, they find it either totally impossible to do or far too easy to bother with. No matter how well you plan and prepare, it is really important to stay flexible during your lessons. Just because you thought something might work well in class, there is no guarantee that it will. It is far better to think on your feet and adapt what you are doing as necessary, rather than to stick to the plan you made just because you made it. This adaptation and flexibility is at the heart of good teaching.

Getting to know your learners

If you want to achieve differentiation in your classroom, then the first job is to get to know your learners. This is why it is harder to differentiate if you teach a large number of learners or if you don't get to spend very much time with each group that you teach – you simply don't get to know as much about them. In an early years setting or a primary school, the practitioner or teacher gets to spend a lot of time with their children over the course of the year. Within the first month of the school year starting, a primary teacher will have already spent more than a hundred hours with their children. The observations and assessments that take place in those first few weeks will help them plan the learning so that it meets the needs of each child. In contrast, secondary teachers and those in the post-compulsory sector may not spend a hundred hours with each learner during an entire school year. This means that it is much more tricky to personalise the learning when working with older learners, and the strategies you use for differentiation will of necessity need to be adapted.

Your ability as a teacher to differentiate for your learners will depend on:

- the amount of time you spend with them
- how much time you have available to do observations or assessments
- how closely you get to observe the learning of different individuals
- how much support you have during lessons from other staff
- the size of the class or group
- the amount of time you have available to plan for different needs.

The process of 'getting to know' your learners happens over time, and if you are only with a class for a short period of time each week, it can feel very hard to get to know them properly. You need to figure out what phase of learning they are in – in different skill areas or different parts of the curriculum. Are they just starting out? Are they gaining in confidence? Are they a high attainer or do they struggle in this subject?

What differences are there?

It is important to remember that academic attainment (what some refer to as 'intelligence', 'ability' or 'achievement') is not the only difference between learners. It may not even be the most important difference between them when it comes to their learning, because there are lots of other factors that can impact on the progress they make in school. Remember too that attainment is not only about achievement in the core subjects – just because an individual struggles with maths does not mean they might not be a high attainer in music. As well as academic factors, the learner's concentration levels, their motivation and their age within the year group can all have a very significant impact on their learning. If a learner is feeling stressed or if they lack confidence this will have a significant impact on their classroom experiences. If there are difficulties in their home life, or if they have undergone some kind of trauma, all this will feed into what happens with their learning.

When you are planning for differentiation, consider how, when and why you might need to take into account the following differences between your learners:

- language backgrounds – including the amount of time they have spent speaking English
- vocabulary acquisition – in terms of its breadth and depth, and also in their conceptual understanding of words
- attention spans and ability to concentrate for extended periods of time
- levels of interest in a subject or topic, or in acquiring a particular skill set
- amount of prior knowledge or experience of a subject or topic
- levels of motivation generally, or in a specific task
- preferred ways of learning, thinking and remembering
- speed of working
- accuracy and speed of handwriting
- chronological age within the year group
- level of maturity in comparison to their peers
- level of physical development in comparison to their peers
- self-confidence and/or self-esteem
- knowledge about and experience of the wider world
- communication skills
- physical needs or difficulties – for instance, sight or hearing problems
- psychological needs or difficulties
- social, cultural and faith backgrounds – including attitudes to education in the home
- upbringing – for instance whether they are a looked-after child, or if they are from a background where they may have moved schools a lot
- medical background – for example, if they were a premature baby, or if they have had a significant amount of time off school because of illness
- any identified SEND
- time spent in education, including the number of settings attended.

For instance, you might have one learner in your class who is newly arrived from overseas, who speaks very little English, but who is fluent in two other languages and is a gifted mathematician. In the same class you might have another learner who has a hearing impairment, who was born prematurely, who is chronologically the youngest in the class, and who has weak literacy skills. And then you might have yet another learner who is a high-flyer from a supportive and stable home background, who speeds through the curriculum, finds whatever learning they are asked to do very easy indeed and tends to quickly become bored. The level of challenge in any single task that you set will vary massively for each of these learners. Giving them all exactly the same thing to do in class, without any adaptation, will of necessity mean that some of them struggle while there is absolutely no stretch or challenge for others. You can only really know about the level of challenge they will experience in a task when you know the individuals themselves.

Going in cold

The hardest kind of differentiation to do is when you go into a session 'cold', knowing nothing at all about the needs and attainment levels of the learners you will be working with. This might be the case on the first day of term, particularly if you haven't had access to any information ahead of time. It is typically the case if you are a supply teacher – you may never have met the class before and indeed you may never meet them again. It can be the case for cover supervisors, and it also happens when I go into schools to do CPD (continuing professional development) sessions with a group of staff that I've not met before. Although I will have been given a bit of context about the school and the needs of the staff before the day, what I won't generally know is anything about the people who actually work there and who will be in my session.

- What do they think and feel about the behaviour of the learners in their school?
- What problems are they experiencing in their classrooms?
- Are there things going on in their personal lives that might add to their levels of stress?
- How well supported do they feel by the leaders of their school?

If I just ignore all these factors and push on regardless with a pre-planned session that takes no account of the context, there may well be a mismatch between my teaching and the learners – just as with your learners. This is not to say that I haven't planned what I am going to cover, but it is to say that I can and will adapt what I'm doing as I go along, to try to match it to their learning needs.

When you go into a session cold, you can still differentiate, but you need to think on your feet in order to do so. You have to find ways to get a feel for the group very quickly and to respond to the information you receive in a flexible manner. Think ahead of time about how you can find things out from the group, planning activities that will allow you to do this. Think also about how you might adapt your planned teaching activities to better suit them, if they don't seem to fit with what the group needs to learn. In a situation where you don't yet know the learners well, whether at the start of the school year or as a temporary teacher, it can be useful to:

- **Do some kind of 'getting to know you' activity:** For instance, when I'm working with a group of teachers, one of the very first things I often do is to ask them to help me figure out who is the rebel in the room. This helps me to break the ice and get a feel for both who is happy to put themselves forward and who has the potential to be a bit rebellious in my session. (I love the rebels – I need them to make my sessions run as well as possible!) Similarly, if you are a cover supervisor or a supply teacher, you might ask the class to tell who is best at the subject you are teaching them, because you are going to need their help during the lesson. This approach usefully puts the power in the hands of the learners, and lets them see that you are going to be responsive to their needs.
- **Set some information or idea-gathering activities so that you can find out how much knowledge the learners already have:** I tend to set short group discussions, so that I can move around the room listening in to conversations and getting a feel for what the groups currently think. When I listen in to groups, I stand back a bit rather than moving in too close, as this can tend to put people off from what they are saying, especially if they don't know you very well. A quick quiz or straw poll, using a show of hands to get answers, works well to gain a feel for the group. For example, I use a 'how many years of experience do you have?' activity when I'm working with teachers. Similarly, you could do a 'what's your favourite subject?' straw poll, to get a feel for likely attitudes to the lesson, in a classroom situation.
- **At the start of your time together, ask the group to write down what they want to find out, change, or know about, as a result of your time together:** I get teachers to write their thoughts down on a sticky note when I begin working with them. I then flick through these notes whenever I get a chance during the day, so that I can get a feel for what it is the group wants to find out about. I adapt my sessions as I go along, to ensure that I focus on their main concerns. Then I use the sticky notes as a plenary at the end of the day, to help them analyse the strategies they have learnt to deal with their concerns. Again, this helps the learners to see that I am going to be responsive to their specific needs, rather than imposing a pre-existing set of ideas on them.

Remember that you can't perform miracles – if you're only going to be with a class for a short period of time, it won't be possible to meet the needs of every single individual in it. (That is difficult enough to do even when you are with them long term.)

However, where you can put strategies in place to at least find out what the learners want to know, you are more likely to engage with them and help them to learn something new.

Before you begin

When you know ahead of time who you are going to be teaching, there are a number of things that you can do to gather information about the likely needs of your learners. As the saying goes, 'knowledge is power' – the more you know, the better you can plan for differentiation. At the same time, it would be a mistake to make too many assumptions before you meet a group of learners for the first time, particularly around their behaviour and likely attitude. Some individuals and classes get themselves a reputation early on in their school careers, and this hangs around them like a bad smell, and can become a self-fulfilling prophecy. When teachers come to know some learners as 'the tricky ones' or 'the ones who can't be bothered', this can subconsciously affect our approach and expectations.

Despite this caveat, it is very much worth doing a bit of preparation before you meet your learners for the first time. You could:

- look to see what information is already on file about them – for instance, any SEND assessments that have been done previously, and any EHCPs (education and health care plans) for individual learners
- arrange a meeting to have a chat with the SENDCo (special educational needs and disabilities coordinator) about any learners who have been identified as having SEND
- look at samples of learning from previous year groups – a quick glance through some old exercise books could give you valuable insights
- view a portfolio with samples of work sent over from a previous school – for instance, some schools pass this over on the transition from primary to secondary, and at the preschool I help to run we pass on the children's 'learning journeys'
- check the results of assessments, tests or exams your new learners have done in the past
- get information about any problems with attendance and punctuality rates
- talk to their previous teachers – if you work in a secondary school, you may have the opportunity to talk to the primary teachers about your new Year 7s in the summer term before they arrive; if you work in a primary school, you should hopefully get the chance to liaise with the children's early years settings before the start of the year
- ask their parents or carers for information – remember, parents are the ones who know the most about their own children

- if possible, do a home visit to get to know more about the family – if your school doesn't yet use home visits, suggest it as a possibility
- ask the learners themselves to send you a letter telling you a bit about themselves, and about their hopes, wishes and expectations for the year – my children were asked to write a letter to the head teacher on their transition to secondary school.

We should take care not to form assumptions based on what we read and hear before we meet a class, particularly about a learner's attitudes to learning. It is perfectly possible for a learner to change their approach, or the learner's approach to have been influenced by factors that no longer apply. It is also perfectly possible for educators to make sweeping assumptions about attainment or attitude, or for us to fail to see that problematic behaviour is masking an unidentified and unmet need. If you are ever told that an individual or a class is 'the awkward/difficult one', make sure to give them the chance for a fresh start, especially in your first meeting. While there is often some truth in the label, every learner deserves a fresh start and a chance to prove themselves.

A letter from home

Learners can find it hard to express their thoughts, ideas, opinions or feelings in a school situation – they might feel awkward about telling you what they really think, or not know quite how best to express what they are feeling. One way to get past this issue, and to really get to know your new learners, is to ask their parents or carers to drop you a short note to tell you about their child. This is particularly valuable for the youngest children, especially on their first entry into an early years setting or a primary school. With very young children, who are unlikely to be able to put these kinds of things into words for you, the parents and carers are a great source of knowledge and information about their own child. The personal insights they provide – 'he's absolutely terrified of spiders', 'she often gets tearful when her dad's away for work', 'he's been very unsettled since his grandma died last month' – can prove invaluable in knowing what activities will support the individual's learning, and which ones to definitely avoid.

Obviously not all parents would have the time or the inclination to write a letter for you. However, even if only a handful of parents respond, it will still give you an insight into your learners that you would never otherwise have got. Even though they might not know as much as you about teaching and learning, a learner's parents/carers really are the people who know their child the best. They certainly understand their own child's foibles and how the child might react to a new environment. Explain to parents and carers that the letter from home is not meant to be about academic attainment, or about what the learner has done well in at school in previous years. What you are interested in finding out about is the unique qualities of the learner – what they are really interested in, what upsets them or worries them, whether there is anything they would really hate if you asked them to do it, what activities they love most. Although this approach is best suited to the parents and carers of younger children, there is no reason at all why you should not use this idea with older learners as well. As an added benefit you would get a feel for which parents and carers are most likely to be supportive of your efforts with their child at school.

Home visits

A fantastic way to get to know your new learners is to visit them at home before or soon after they start with you. If you really want an insight into 'where your learners come from', what better than the opportunity to see where they spend most of their time? A home visit also offers a great chance to support each individual's transition into a new setting because you can share information about what it is like with the learner and their parents/carers. The learner also gets to meet some members of staff before they even begin, which gives them some familiar faces to look out for when they start at your setting. Typically, home visits will take place in the Foundation Stage – before a child begins at an early years setting, or before they enter their first nursery or Reception class in school. Home visits are not statutory – at our setting we offer them as an option for parents and carers, but there should be absolutely no compulsion on parents or carers to take up the offer. During a home visit, you could:

- ask if the parents/carers have any questions, or if they need any support with filling out any forms that they need to complete to register at your setting
- encourage the parents/carers to give you useful information about languages spoken at home, things that the child particularly enjoys or worries about, and so on
- talk with the parents/carers about any concerns they might have as to how their child will settle into your setting, or with their general development
- explain about the policies that are in place in your setting, and answer any questions the parents/carers might have about these
- show the child some photos of the setting and take along some toys to share and play with, so that the child becomes familiar with what will be on offer

Transition

Potentially, a lot of information and knowledge about learners can get lost at the transition points, whether from an early years setting into a primary school, a primary school into a secondary school, or a secondary school into a college. The learners move from a setting where at least some of the staff know them really well, to a new place where no one knows them at all. In fact, much the same can happen on the move from one year group in a school to another, especially in larger organisations where it is tricky for staff to find enough time to communicate with each other. The more methods we can find to pass on the knowledge we have about our learners, the less chance there will be that the next teacher has to start all over again from scratch.

It is useful to see transition as a long-term project, rather than something that happens once a year when the learners all 'move up' to a new class or school. Where it is possible for settings in a locality to work together over several years, this has a powerful impact on how well you can get to know the learners who will be coming to you at a later date, and consequently how you might plan for the different things that they need. Staff can share information and knowledge with each other, and learners gain a sense of continuity and cohesion between the different settings. In order to support learners in the transition, you could:

- **Devise ways for settings in your locality to work in conjunction with each other:** For instance, this could be via shared projects such as sports events, performances or festivals that feature children from various feeder schools.
- **Share venues with each other:** For instance, our local secondary school hosts a dance festival where all the local primaries take part, and our local primary school uses our preschool hall for school shows.
- **Build in allocated time for teachers and support staff to communicate with each other before, during and after transitions:** The value of doing this should far outweigh the costs involved.
- **Find the most useful ways to pass on information:** Talk to colleagues about what they find best and most helpful – marks, grades, notes, discussions, samples of learning, etc.
- **Highlight any learners who have particular needs on transition:** This is especially important for those whose needs might not be obvious at first.
- **Ensure the smooth handover of information about SEND:** Include any plans that have already been made for the appropriate differentiation of provision.
- **Create transition books for the learners to take with them:** This is particularly useful for learners who have SEND.
- **Make a 'passport' for the learners to take on to their new school:** In it, give a brief summary of all that you know about them.

When a learner has SEND, it can be very useful for them to have additional visits to their new setting, in order to feel comfortable with it. You might help them create a photo booklet of the new setting, to help them begin to come to terms with the changes that are going to happen. A useful alternative is for them to make a video on their visits to your setting. When you know that a learner with SEND is coming to your setting, it may be possible to plan for differentiation before they arrive. For example, at our pre-school we knew that a child with a disability was going to be joining us, several months before the child started with us. This meant that we could audit our provision, adapt the physical layout of our setting to ensure the child could access it, plan for how we could meet the child's needs and apply for additional funding from the local authority.

As well as the major transitions from one setting to another, transitions also occur while a learner is in the same school. As they move up through the year groups, it is easy for information to get lost, or for expectations to be accidentally lowered. A lovely way to overcome this issue is to ask each learner to choose an excellent piece of work towards the end of the year (perhaps one per subject). The piece of work they select should be one that they feel demonstrates their full capabilities to their new teacher or teachers. The next teacher could either flick through the set of samples to see what the learners are capable of when working at their best, or alternatively the examples could be stuck in the front of the learner's new exercise books, to remind them of their starting point. This helps give the message of shared high expectations between staff in the school.

Lesson plans

The way that you plan on paper for differentiation will vary according to the needs of your class and also according to the kind of format that your school asks you to use (if this is specified). Some schools require very detailed planning, in a specific format, and teachers are sometimes asked to hand this in to senior leaders to check over ahead of the lessons. Other schools are much less rigid in their approach, and will allow for a good deal of individuality in the planning process. Generally speaking, the best lesson plan for differentiation is one that works for an individual teacher, both in thinking through a lesson ahead of time, and in referring to the plan during it. As teachers gain in experience, they tend to be able to manage with less in the way of detailed planning, particularly when they have taught the same or similar lessons before. However, as the learners to whom the lesson is going to be taught change, it is important to think about how the techniques for differentiation used within the lesson should change as well.

There are many different ways to set out a lesson plan to include differentiation:

- You could have a separate box marked 'differentiation', where you identify the specifics of the differentiation you will do.
- You might separate out differentiated resources, support and tasks and identify specific individuals who will have access to each of these.

- You might highlight the objectives that you wish certain individuals to achieve during the lesson.
- You could make a list of key words and terms that you want everyone to understand, highlighting a few of the more complex ones that will really stretch and challenge your high attainers.
- You could use some kind of code to identify the learners with SEND or EAL (English as an additional language) in a group, and write notes about the strategies you will use for them.

Above all else, though, your plan needs to be usable in the lesson rather than so detailed that it is hard for you to refer to it.

Questions for consideration

It is useful to see the process of writing a lesson plan as part of the thinking that goes on before a lesson, rather than a blueprint for exactly what must happen within it. By mapping out what you aim for the learners to learn, and the kind of activities you plan to include, this will help you think about whether the content is appropriate for all your learners. Of course, it's important to remember that you won't always (or even often) have time to go into lots and lots of detailed thinking about differentiation for specific individuals. However, if you do at least ask yourself some questions, some of the time, you will put yourself into the right mindset for differentiation.

To get you to think about the type of planning that would work best for you and your class or classes, you could consider some of the following questions:

- How and when in the lesson can I find out what prior knowledge or skills my learners already have on this topic?
- Which specific learners do I feel I might most need or want to differentiate for in this lesson?
- What is the central skill, concept or knowledge that I want all learners to grasp during this lesson?
- Are there any of my learners who have already achieved this, or who might struggle to get to this point during the lesson?
- Practically, how am I going to stretch or support these learners at the same time as teaching the main body of the lesson?
- Am I going to separate out my expectations of what different learners should learn by the end of this lesson?
- Am I going to separate out the tasks that different learners will be expected to do?

- Will there be any element of choice for my learners during this lesson?
- How many different levels of complexity am I going to plan into this lesson?
- How will I link and match the tasks I use to different levels of understanding or skill?
- Who is going to decide which tasks to do – the teacher or the learners (this could of course be a mix)?
- Are there some individuals for whom I need to plan a completely separate task? (For instance, a new starter to the school who has no spoken or written English at all.)
- Does everyone need to be involved in any whole-class teaching that I am going to do during the lesson?
- If not, how am I going to manage any breakout groups? Do I have someone who can supervise them or will they be able to learn independently?
- Are there any learners who will need one-to-one provision, or who might need to be withdrawn from the lesson to work in a separate group?
- Will there be any opportunities for peer-to-peer learning in this lesson?
- How will I plan for and manage the provision of support and resources?
- How will I identify what I want the learners to know/understand/be able to do/think about during the lesson? Will it be the same for everyone?

The way that you set out your planning, and the method you use to note the strategies for differentiation in it, will depend on the phase you are working in and what you are teaching. If your school does not provide you with a format to use, a quick Internet search throws up a myriad of possibilities. However, it is highly likely that you will need to adapt these, according to your own specific context, setting or needs. Whatever format you use, do make sure that it is easy to refer to during the lesson. In some ways, planning is as much about thinking through what you are going to do, and how well it will work, as about making notes to refer to during a lesson. Bear this in mind at all times, and see any written plan as a template of possibilities, rather than a blueprint.

Example: Planning for differentiation in the early years

Because of the very high ratio of adults to children in the early years setting that I help to run – at least one adult for every five children – we have the opportunity to personalise the learning for each individual. If you're a secondary teacher with 250 different students, then clearly our situation is very different to yours. However, you might be able to draw out some useful thinking points from the way that we go about doing this. The way that we plan at preschool is very different to the way that teachers plan in schools – we don't teach individual classes or lessons, so we don't need or want to write out separate lesson plans. Not all of the children will be in the setting all of the time; some may only attend for a single session, while others are with us all week. Our main goal is to think about how we can plan an environment that will lead to learning for each individual, and to achieve a balance between child- and adult-led activities. We have developed our approach as a team, over several years, and through a process of trial and error, and self-evaluation and reflection. We wanted to make the planning format as useful and easy to refer to as possible, while at the same time ensuring curriculum coverage for each child, and responding to individual needs.

Our staff work on the overall planning for our provision together each week, by making notes directly onto a large working document (A3 size). The document has a box for each of the different areas of continuous provision that we have in our setting, both inside and outside. We operate a freeflow system, where children can move between indoors and outdoors as they wish, so potentially they can cover the curriculum in either or both areas, and so we need to make sure it is resourced to allow that to happen. Staff note on the planning document the resources or activities that are on offer in each area of continuous provision each week. They note whether the activity will be child-initiated, adult-initiated or adult-directed. They also note whether they are going to take a particular focus in an area, for instance on a key skill or theme. Each child has a 'key person', who is responsible for mapping that individual's progress, overseeing what they do and reporting back to parents or carers about how they are getting on. However, all staff can and do chip in to give insights into and information about the different children, including information about their current interests.

In order to plan for differentiation we:

- identify the next steps that each child needs to take in their learning in terms of skills, understanding and knowledge (both academic and social/emotional)
- work out how we can resource and organise our provision in such a way that we help each child achieve these next steps
- scribble notes and make annotations on the planning document when we notice something specific about an individual's learning – for instance, we might note that a child is interested in a specific topic at the moment, or identify an area of skill or knowledge that needs developing next

- respond to these annotations – either by adapting the resources in the moment, or by adapting the way that we set out the provision the next time the child is in the setting
- check for full coverage of the curriculum, using the child's learning journey portfolio as a basis for assessment
- note the balance of child-initiated and adult-initiated learning that is going on.

For instance, if we observed that a child was taking a great interest in water play, but that they still needed to do lots of work on counting and mathematical language, we might set up the water play area with lots of different sized containers and with some foam number shapes. Practitioners could then talk with the child about the size of the containers, counting with the child as they are filled up. The practitioners would use language such as 'how much', 'how many', 'the most' and so on, as well as counting how many containers there are, identifying the numbers in the water, and so on. In this way, you can capitalise on the child's interests to ensure engagement and motivation, and incorporate the next steps for learning at the same time.

Approaches to differentiated planning

When it comes to differentiation, there is no one right way to do it. Often, your differentiation will be made up of a host of different and subtle strategies that combine together to meet the needs of the learners in your class. What works for children of one age might not work for older learners; the methods that are effective for teaching one subject might not be the best approach for teaching another. You won't always get differentiation perfect, by any means – if there is such a thing. Below are some starting points for thinking about the approaches to differentiation that you might take when you are planning your lessons. You will find lots more detail about what and how you can differentiate in the following sections of this book.

Planning to the top

One approach to differentiated planning is to decide on the content, ideas or skills that you want your highest-attaining learners to achieve, and then to figure out the kinds of support you need to put in place for other learners to achieve these things as well. This is sometimes referred to as 'teaching to the top'. This approach could work well in some subjects or lessons (for instance, those in which you are teaching lots of factual content). The support that you put in place could be:

- additional adult input – for instance, the teacher working with a specific group who need extra input
- extra resources that only some of the learners need (for instance, a key word list or a writing scaffold
- giving extra time to the learners who most need it.

However, in a lesson in which learning a skill is the main focus, planning or teaching to the top may not be appropriate. When we are teaching a specific skill, it is often the case that some learners have already got that skill under their belts, while others have not begun to grasp it at all. A good example of this would be the difference between a learner who understands perfectly how to use speech marks and one who doesn't. There is not much point in re-teaching the use of speech marks to those learners who already know how to use this punctuation mark correctly. It would be a much better use of those learners' time to set them a different task, such as asking them to write some sentences or stories that have speech marks in them, or to focus on a different punctuation mark entirely. That way you can focus the teaching on those learners who actually need to learn or master the basic skill. How we go about doing this is the tricky bit and perhaps this is why we tend to resort to whole-class teaching, even when we know that for some learners what we are doing is basically repeating something they already know. Of course, there is no harm in occasionally revisiting a skill or topic, but if we do so repeatedly we run the risk of them disengaging from the learning.

Topping and tailing

Another approach to planning for differentiation is to figure out what level you know or would expect the main body of the learners to be at already, and then to think about a support for those below this level, and an extension for those above it – what I like to call 'topping and tailing your planning'. Where you can't spare lots of time to plan for differentiation in detail, this offers a good alternative, because it makes you think about both a potential support and a possible extension or challenge. Even if you just think this through, rather than writing it out in your lesson plan in lots of detail, it will help you consider potential strategies for differentiation.

The 'tail' task will tend to be something that offers more support or scaffolding for the learners, while the 'top' task will be something that creates a challenge – for instance, an added level of complexity.

As an example, we can return to the lesson on speech marks:

- The 'top' task might be to turn examples of indirect speech into dialogue, using correct punctuation.
- The 'tail' task might be to add speech marks back into some dialogue that has been written out already.

The three column method

As well as using the 'top and tail' approach for lesson activities, you can also use it to create differentiated worksheets, with your 'tail' task on the left side and your 'top' task on the right. For instance, imagine you want to create a page of maths problems for your learners to work on. Divide the page of your worksheet into three columns:

- **The middle column** has problems that are at the expected level, i.e. the level that you think is going to be about right for the majority of the class. Ask all the learners to attempt at least one or two problems from this column to see how they get on. Encourage them to think about whether the middle column problems are too easy or too difficult for them. This kind of metacognition (thinking about their own thinking in relation to learning) is very useful for them.
- **The column to the left** has problems that are at a level below the expected level – these are often problems requiring less abstract thought, or with a lower level of complexity, because these are easier to solve. If learners struggle doing the problems in the middle column, they should move to the left and work through the problems here.
- **The column to the right** has problems that are at a level above the expected level – usually requiring more abstraction or more complex thinking. If learners find the middle column easy, or get all the middle column problems right, they should move to the problems in the right-hand column.

You might also leave a fourth, blank column as a 'top' task, where learners can create their own sums or problems if they manage to complete the third column. They could then give these to a classmate to complete.

Increasing complexity

When we are playing a video game, as we progress through the levels, the game makers add more characters, new situations and fresh puzzles for us to solve. The increase in complexity maintains our interest in the game and pushes us to extend our learning within the game-world scenario. In a similar way, you can add more complexity to lesson tasks to make them more interesting and gradually more challenging for your learners to complete. For instance, if your learners were doing a piece of writing, the complexity might build in terms of:

- the number of words used in each sentence
- the length of the words being used
- the complexity of the thinking behind the vocabulary that is used – i.e. how abstract it is or the kind of terminology that is included
- the punctuation that is used

- the complexity of the different sentence types – for instance, a rhetorical question would be trickier to devise than a normal question
- the amount of development given to each idea.

There are lots of ways that you can vary and build the complexity of tasks. You might do this by adapting:

- the sophistication of the research required from learners in order to complete the task
- how open-ended the question is that is being asked and answered
- the perspectives and viewpoints you ask the learner to adopt during the activity
- the amount of inference that is required to work out what is going on
- the level of abstraction of the concepts that have to be handled during the task
- the amount of detail that is to be included in the response to the question
- the make-up of the group that the learners work in to complete the task.

Different timings

Another way to plan for differentiation is to plan to give your learners varied amounts of time to work on the same activity or to listen to the same content. This allows you to push some learners to move quickly through the content of a lesson, and to give more time to those who find an activity harder to understand or complete. You might decide for yourself how much time you want different groups of learners to have on a task, but you could also ask the learners themselves to work out how long they need. It is really useful to encourage your learners to set their own targets and to reflect on which approaches to learning work best for them – this kind of metacognitive activity is closely linked to good outcomes. When learners understand how to manage their own time, this forms a good basis for later academic success (for instance, when revising for exams, or when writing essays).

Circus of activities

Sometimes you want a class of learners to do a variety of activities during a lesson. This is an ideal opportunity to create a 'circus' – a circuit in which the learners complete several different activities on the same topic in turn. For instance, in a science lesson you might have a series of five tasks that all show the same scientific concept at work, but in different ways. The learners work their way around the stations, doing an experiment at each one and then answering questions on it. The questions could be differentiated from green (easy) to red (hard). The learners could answer as many questions as possible in a set time limit, be challenged to answer the question that they feel is at the right level for them, or be asked to complete at least one green, one amber and one red question.

Worksheets

Although worksheets sometimes get a bad press, in fact they can be a helpful way for you to support learners who are significantly behind or ahead of the rest of the class in their learning. One of the useful things about worksheets is that a lot of thought and forward planning can go into the creation of them, so that you can aim for the tasks to be at exactly the right level for individual learners. Bear in mind that it does not just have to be about the tasks or the content being different; you could differentiate a worksheet by using a larger font for a learner who has a sight impairment, or by highlighting the key words in bold for an EAL learner.

Another useful facet of worksheets is that you can create a single 'master' document, and then adapt this for learners who need something slightly or significantly different – either as a support or as an extension. You can also reuse and share the materials that you have made, again adapting these to suit new contexts. Additionally, if you stay in teaching long enough, you will find that certain topics or subjects come back around and you can then update and reuse your old worksheets. (A good example of this is the fact that the Shakespeare plays *Romeo and Juliet* and *Macbeth* are now appearing as GCSE set texts – I originally taught them when they were set for Year 9 SATs, which have long since bitten the dust, but I still have my old worksheets in a file.)

To adapt a worksheet to suit the needs of different learners, you might:

- add images or symbols to support a learner who is new to English
- put the instructions in two languages – in the learner's home language as well as in English
- create a word bank in a box to help learners who need access to additional vocabulary to complete the task
- create a key word bank with supporting images, to help learners with very little English
- create a word bank with a list of key word definitions, to help learners who might struggle with understanding some of the words
- use a simplified version of a text for a learner who is behind the rest of the class with their reading
- enlarge the font size for a learner who has a visual impairment

- give some additional, more complex questions for learners who you know will complete the worksheet easily
- add some links for reading or research, to use as an extension task.

We tend to think that we would always need to make several different worksheets in order to differentiate properly for different groups of learners in a class. At the very least we might think that we would have to adapt a single worksheet before it could suit different learners. However, you can also use the same worksheet with a whole class, and still find ways to differentiate it. For instance:

- Some learners are asked to aim to complete half the questions in a set time, while others are asked to complete them all – a good way to set half the questions is to tell learners to choose either even-numbered or odd-numbered questions.
- Fold the worksheet in half so that the learner doesn't feel overwhelmed by the amount of writing or the number of tasks that are on it. Ask them to complete half of the worksheet first, and come to you to check how they have got on before moving on to the second half.
- Challenge and empower your learners by using 'you choose' – they decide which bit of the worksheet they are going to complete first, how many questions they are going to answer in a given time frame, or in what order they are going to complete the tasks.

Using learners' interests

We sometimes complain that learners just can't seem to remember anything, and yet we all know just how much they can retain when it is about something that is of interest to them. They will learn the spelling and statistics of a hundred different dinosaurs, or memorise the name and team of every single footballer in the premier league. They will know everything there is to know about every Pokémon creature that has ever been invented, or the name and full details of every character featured in the entire Harry Potter series. When they are learning about something that is of interest to them, they tend to approach it with incredibly high levels of motivation.

Obviously school can't always be about things that are of interest to the learners, but it is often possible for you, the teacher, to create a situation where you mirror an area of the learners' interests in the learning that you do. For instance, say you wanted to develop a project in which the learners created a product and then sold it, in order to learn about how businesses work, about packaging and marketing, or to develop mathematical understanding around sales and profit. Although the areas to be learnt about would usually be specified by the teacher, the focus of the business could be linked to the learners' interests. For instance, a learner who was keen on football could create and sell a football-related product, while a learner who loved animals could link their project to that, perhaps devising and selling a new design of animal carrier.

Projects

Projects can offer a useful way to differentiate, and they give the opportunity for considerable depth in learning, because they can so easily be linked to what the learners are interested in. The great thing about projects is that they can be tailored to the learners' interests, and this helps the learners feel more engaged with what they are learning – their motivation levels stay naturally high. When learners have an element of choice in the topic they are being asked to study, they tend to invest more of themselves in their work. Projects are fantastic for encouraging your high attainers to stretch themselves and they give your strugglers a chance to shine as well, showing you what they can do when it's about a subject that is close to their hearts. Projects allow the teacher to bring a sense of the real world to the classroom, showing their learners how the learning they do in class relates to the world beyond the school gates. By sharing their project work with their peers in class, your learners can help you cover learning in a variety of topics, or in a range of subjects within one topic area.

Having said all this, the demands of the present curriculum mean that you may only be able to find limited time for project work. Projects will also need careful management by the teacher to ensure that the learners stay focused and on track with their timing, and to ensure that there is sufficient depth and breadth to the learning. As with any method for teaching and learning, careful planning is needed to ensure that all learners get the maximum benefit. Some learners will need a lot more support than others, which is where differentiation comes in. Doing a project is not just about academic attainment; it is about organisational skills as well. In fact, one of the key learning experiences learners take from doing a project is about organising their time and staying focused. You will need to think carefully about how your learners will be able to access the most appropriate resources to complete the research for their projects. For older learners it might be useful to create a shared online space where you can leave documents, articles, reading lists and so on for them to use for research.

In many ways, as a format, projects are naturally differentiated, because they relate to a learner's area of interest and prior knowledge, and because they can be completed to different levels. The outcomes you get will vary according to the approach and prior knowledge of the learner – in other words, differentiation by outcome. However, you can also use strategies to increase the levels of differentiation in project work as it proceeds. For instance, you might adapt:

- **The choice of topics:** Are you going to specify a theme or a subject area around which the project must be based, or will you leave it completely up to the learners to decide what their project will be about? Some learners may struggle to cope with a completely open-ended choice but could respond well to a choice of two or three options, so do you need to take this into account and differentiate for it? You might also offer your learners a set of choices that will help them target areas of weakness in their learning.
- **The planning methods by which the projects are done:** For instance, you might need to create scaffolds or workbooks for some of your learners to use, especially for those who struggle to organise their approach and manage their time. Other learners might be given a more open-ended challenge.
- **The targets you set:** For instance, are these going to be time-limited, or about the amount of work that you expect to be completed by certain points in a specific time frame? Encourage your learners to get involved in setting their own targets, and keeping themselves on track.
- **The amount of support you offer to each learner:** You could develop a set of section headings for one learner, working together to find the right format. You could leave others to decide how to structure the work for themselves. You might ask a TA (teaching assistant) to work with one particular group who you know most needs support.
- **The materials that you have available for learners to use:** For example, you might need to bring in some specific books suited to particular learners, or you could highlight websites that you think it would be useful for different learners to access.
- **The approach to research:** You might need to teach the skills required for your learners to do this well. For instance, do some of them need to learn how to use a contents page or an index? Do others need to understand how to summarise information? You could teach these skills in 'mini lessons' during the course of the project (see page 22 for more on this technique).
- **Whether learners work individually or in groups:** You may also want to consider whether the decision about working alone or in particular groups will be up to you or left to the learners to decide.
- **If learners do work in groups, how you will organise these:** Will the groupings be free choice or teacher-devised? How will it be decided who takes on what role within each group? Can you add challenge by asking learners to work outside of their usual comfort zone when it comes to the role they take on?

Projects tend to take place over an extended period of time, and this means that it is important for the learners to understand how to manage their workload. Support your learners by offering them a structure within which to organise their learning. You might:

- set them a target for how many pages they should complete in a specific time period
- set a goal for how many words or lines they must write in each lesson
- give them a list of tasks and ask them to do a set number of these each week
- ask to have sight of a specific amount of material in each lesson or at the end of a set time period.

Consider asking some or all of your learners to submit part of the project before the end of the time period during which you are working on it, or ask them to show you their progress at specific points over this time. This will help avoid any last-minute panic over work that was not done when it should have been. You can also give them helpful feedback on what they have done so far. This feedback could come from you as their teacher, or the whole class could give them input, critique and advice.

Mini lessons

One of the issues with project work is that the learners might need support in getting hold of the knowledge or skills that they need to complete the task. Another concern that teachers can have is whether the learners will be able to push themselves and create a sufficient level of challenge when they are not interacting directly with the teacher. In order to support the development of knowledge, skills and understanding during project work, you can incorporate 'mini lessons' into the learning time. These are short periods of direct teaching – a bit like a mini lecture – to help you pass on the knowledge or skills that the learners need in order to direct and complete their project work effectively. You could:

- give mini lessons or short lectures to the whole class – if everyone is working on the same project or needs a boost in the same skill set
- offer mini lessons to a small group that needs them – on a specific topic, while the others continue working on their projects
- create learning stations (a bit like topic tables) – where you set out resources related to the topic being studied for the learners to use in their research
- set 'flipped learning' homeworks – in which you specify materials that you want the learners to read, relating to their projects.

Another way to incorporate mini lessons is to set up some 'meet the expert' times, relating to the topic in question. Invite experts into your lessons to talk to the learners – these could be parents who work in a particular field that you are studying, local business people or invited experts such as an author or artist. You could also 'meet' and interview some of your experts via a platform such as Skype, if they are not able to visit the school.

Home/expert groups

When you want a project or other research-style activity to be done in groups, it can be a useful approach to get different learners to work on different parts of a topic for a period of time, before pooling the information that they have collected. A great way to do this is to use home/expert groups. With this approach, learners work together to develop expertise in an area of a subject, then they take back their expertise to share with their original group. As well as being a lot of fun, this technique can also help you to differentiate for your less confident learners, by encouraging them to gather and then share their ideas in a group situation. To use the home/expert group method:

- Decide on a topic or project that you want the learners to study or research, such as volcanoes in geography.
- Split the topic into the different areas that you want to cover, for instance:
  - formation of volcanoes
  - types of volcano
  - volcanoes of the world
  - famous volcanic eruptions
  - geographical impact of eruptions.
- Next, divide up the class into home groups with the same number of members in each group as there are topic headings – for instance, in the example above you would need five learners in each group.
- Ask each group to nominate one person as their 'expert' for each of the five areas – this could be via self-nominations, or they could use a group vote if they prefer. It might be that you decide to nominate the experts yourself, to ensure that certain individuals have the chance to develop specific skills or areas of knowledge.
- The 'experts' now leave their home group and join up with the other chosen 'experts' in their field, to research their part of the topic in detail together.
- When they have had a specified amount of time to do their research, the experts go back to their home group to report back on what they have found out. The group as a whole then decides how to present all their new-found accumulated expertise in the form of a 'volcanoes' presentation or project.

This method is a great way to ensure that everyone contributes to a group activity, and to help your learners learn how to research a new topic. It is also a good way to encourage quieter and less confident learners to get involved in giving their ideas.

Next steps and mastery

The concept of 'next steps' is firmly embedded into planning practice in EYFS (Early Years Foundation Stage),which runs from birth to age five in England. The idea behind the next steps approach is that you identify what the child currently knows and/or can do, and then you figure out which bit of knowledge or skill they need to acquire next, in the different areas of learning of the Foundation Stage. This includes developmental, social and emotional early learning goals, which lead to growing independence and self-care, as well as goals around progression across the curriculum. For instance, if a child is secure in counting up to five, the logical next step would be for them to learn to count up to ten. If a child can already put their shoes on unaided, their next step may be to learn how to put on their coat and do up the buttons. This way of thinking can be very useful as a model for differentiation higher up the education system.

As children progress through the education system, the building blocks for more complex learning are being formed, and if any of the early stages gets missed, this can lead to problems later on. This is where the idea of 'mastery' comes in, particularly in subjects such as maths. The idea is that learners need to understand (or 'master') early concepts, such as place value, before they can move on to grasp more complex ones. At the earliest stages of learning, it is reasonably straightforward to figure out what the next steps will be, so long as you understand which bit of early conceptual knowledge or skill builds on what. There is not much point in asking a child to learn how to do up her laces if she has not yet learnt to put her shoes on the right feet. You cannot expect a learner to learn how to add and subtract until they understand that numbers symbolically 'stand for' an amount of something. As learning gets more complex and complicated, it can be harder to figure out a pathway through it, but it is still really useful to think through what builds on what.

You can get a good sense of how the next steps work for the birth-to-five-years age group by looking at the incredible breadth of skills, attitudes and knowledge outlined in the Early Education guidance: *Development Matters in the Early Years Foundation Stage (EYFS)* available to download at www.foundationyears.org.uk/files/2012/03/Development-Matters-FINAL-PRINT-AMENDED.pdf.

When working with older learners, the concept of 'next steps' offers a useful way to get them to conceptualise their own learning, and to set themselves targets for improvements. Ask them to consider what 'next step' they need to take in their learning in order to get better in a particular subject or technique.

Differentiated groupings

Although we might have 30 different learners in a single class, it would be impossible to differentiate for every single one of them. This is one of the reasons why teachers will often use grouping to support differentiation. We want to try to ensure that the tasks are at the right level for as many of the learners as possible. In theory, grouping the learners will help us to do this because it allows us to offer different tasks to learners, according to their needs. The teacher or school might create a 'high-attaining' group/class that is given harder work, or a 'support group/class' that gets extra input from an additional member of staff, or that gets the majority of the teacher's focus during the lesson.

Remember that groupings are not the same as group work. There is a difference between grouping the learners for ease of differentiation (i.e. so that you get them to do the same work) and the learners actually working on a group activity in a group. In other words, just because the learners are sitting together at a table, does not mean that they are working together as a group. You might sit a group of learners together who you think will all need similar support, but the learners can still work on the task individually, while you give them the input they need. Think carefully about which of these options you are after before you plan how your groupings should work. Do you want them to actually do group work, or are you just sitting them in a group to make teaching them easier?

When grouping for differentiation, you will need to consider the purpose behind the groupings. Are the groupings about clustering learners together according to your understanding of the level of difficulty of the work you want them to do, or is there another purpose behind your use of the approach, such as giving them role models or building their self-confidence? Your groupings might be:

- **Attainment based:** Separating out learners with different levels of attainment in a particular subject, topic or skill, perhaps so that you can give each group a different task.
- **Needs based:** Grouping together the learners who have a specific need for you to address, for example those who need help in building vocabulary or those who need support in the use of English as an additional language.
- **Diversity based:** For some tasks, you might want your focus to be on ensuring that the learners mix in a particular way to share their ideas – for

instance, sharing of ideas between genders, or between learners who have different life experiences.

- **Roles based:** Specifying the roles that the learners will take on within those groupings. For instance, who will be the chair, who the researcher, and so on? Depending on the context, the roles you give could be based on what a learner can already do well, or what they still need to develop.
- **Interest based:** You could simply put together learners who have the same interests, for instance, so that they can work on the same project.
- **Mixed attainment:** Mixing up the learners so that the higher-attaining learners can learn from the lower ones, and vice versa. Remember that what the learners learn will not just be academic – they will develop their social and emotional skills when working in groups as well.
- **Vertical:** Creating groups that have learners of different ages in them – for instance, a group in which your Year 6 learners work with Year 1 children.

If you are using group work, as opposed to simply sitting the learners in a group format, the learners might stay in groups for the whole lesson – for instance, if they were devising and performing some drama presentations. However, you might also wish to use group work for part of the lesson and/or for some specific learners. For instance:

1. You spend a period of time working on a text or other learning stimulus with the whole class.
2. During this whole-class time you ensure that everyone understands the text, you identify any tricky vocabulary and help everyone to understand what all the words in the text mean.
3. You then model the activity (or activities) that you want the class to do related to the text.
4. Next you divide up the class into groups to complete the activity.
5. Some of the groups work independently from the teacher, sharing ideas as a group before moving on to complete an individual task.
6. Other groups have direct input from the teacher or a member of support staff and work through the tasks together with the adults.

Attainment groupings versus mixed groupings

There is no single 'correct' way to group your learners for differentiation – so much will depend on the subject being taught, the type of class you are working with, the phase you teach in, the amount of time your learners tend to spend in groups during lessons, and so on. However, it is important to understand the different potential impacts on the learners from the way that you group them. It is tempting to believe that the closer the learners are in their level of attainment in a subject, the easier you will be able to meet their needs. This assumption is worth challenging.

On the plus side, attainment groupings can …

- ✔ make it easier for the teacher to differentiate by task
- ✔ allow the teacher to use a single set of activities to teach a single class (for instance, with a 'top set' in a secondary school)
- ✔ offer stretch and challenge to your highest-attaining learners
- ✔ allow you to direct support and/or experienced staff where they will make most difference.

However, on the downside, attainment groupings may …

- ✘ cause learners to label themselves as 'failing' and consequently cause a decrease in motivation
- ✘ leave learners stuck in a group that is not appropriate for them, if not enough thought is given to how they might move 'up' or 'down', or if the learners are not assessed accurately in the first place
- ✘ lead to disengagement from those in the lower-attaining groups
- ✘ cause extra pressure, or the perception of it, on those in the higher-attaining groups.

On the plus side, mixed groupings can …

- ✔ enable lower attainers to be 'pulled up' by those who attain more highly, by offering them a model of what higher attainment looks like
- ✔ help to ensure that learners do not develop a closed mindset about their potential
- ✔ ease any pressures caused by a learner's perceptions of their own ability in a subject.

However, on the downside, these groupings may …

- ✘ make it more complex for the teacher to differentiate by task
- ✘ mean that you have to think more about differentiating activities for different learners
- ✘ cause you to spread the available support more thinly around the group.

Bear in mind that, even if you don't tell the learners what attainment group they are in, they are likely to be able to work this out for themselves. Nor are parents easily fooled, even if you think that your group names don't give anything away, perhaps particularly in a primary class where parents often know each other's children outside of school. It can be a good idea to keep your groupings moving around – a flexible approach works well to ensure that everyone works with everyone and that no one feels like they are 'stuck' in one grouping.

Peer group teaching for differentiation

Although it is the teacher's responsibility to teach (and differentiate for) the learners, you can plan to get the learners themselves involved with supporting and challenging each other's learning as well. Generally speaking, young people are very supportive of their peers, and keen to help them to do well, although this may dissipate a bit as they move into their teenage years. Even if your learners are not supportive of each other, though, it is a good lesson for them for the teacher to insist that they work respectfully with each other. As well as your learners building their social and emotional skills, when they are peer group teaching, asking them to explain something to someone else is a great way to cement and clarify their learning.

You might plan for your learners to work together to:

- scribe for a partner – one person says what they are thinking out loud, while the partner makes notes; they then swap over roles
- give some feedback to their peers to help them grasp a new skill or concept – give a pen to those learners who have grasped what you are doing quickly and ask them to go around the room helping those who haven't
- assess each other's work – for instance, marking a spelling test or giving a 'what works well' (www) and an 'even better if' (ebi) for a piece of writing
- answer an assessment in groups – deciding on the correct answer to each question by discussing it together first
- support learners in a different age group – for instance, Year 5 children reading their favourite stories to Year 1 children.

Learning objectives

One of the central questions when planning for effective differentiation is the question that you ask yourself when planning any unit of learning. *What do I want the learners to be able to do, to know, or to understand as a result of being in this lesson or series of lessons?* If you don't know what you want them to do as an end result of being taught, you will find it hard to figure out how to differentiate for them or to get them to make progress. When you are planning, try to refine your objectives down to a detailed statement, being as specific as you can about what you are after. Your statement might start with phrases such as:

- I want them to be able to...
- I want them to understand that...
- I want them to remember that...
- I want them to remember how to...
- I want them to know how to...
- I want them to know that...
- I want them to think about how...
- I want them to be fluent in...

It is often the case that we try to fit too many objectives into a single period of learning, and we then lose sight of the central aim that we had in mind. What we really need to think about is how we organise the content to make meaning for our learners – how do we make it clear to them what the objective of the lesson is? It can be helpful to frame your learning objective in terms of a big question. Phrasing your objective as a question can help you stimulate curiosity, and it can also help you focus in on the central concepts that underlie the things you are asking the learners to learn. It can work well to share the question you want to answer with the class at the start of the lesson.

Once you have established your central learning objectives, you need to establish which learners you think can achieve these during the lesson, and whether you might need to have a slightly less lofty aim for some, and a slightly more challenging aim for others. It is all very well saying that you are going to teach to the top of the class, but you also need to be realistic about what is achievable in a specific period of time. Remember: just because you have taught it does not mean they have learnt it – complex ideas can take a lot of explanation before all of your learners will grasp them. To give an example, let's say that your learning objective is for your learners to understand the technique and logic behind how and when semicolons are used.

- Some learners might not get beyond an understanding of what is meant by 'an independent clause'.
- Some learners might understand how to write sentences using semicolons by the end of the lesson, but not have fully conceptualised the 'why' behind what they are doing (i.e. that a semicolon can link two ideas more closely together than if they were in two separate sentences).
- Some learners might finish the lesson being able to write sentences where semicolons are used accurately, and understand how they link two ideas, but they might not be able to use them consistently and spontaneously in their own writing.

- Some learners might end the lesson with a full grasp of semicolons, why they are used and how to use them in the appropriate way in their writing without needing to be prompted.

This is where it might sometimes be useful to split your learning objectives into something like the classic 'all, most, some' categories. The idea of splitting up your objectives in this way has fallen out of favour in recent years, because it can tend to put a ceiling on what we ask learners to achieve. For instance, a learner might feel that they can get away with doing less, on the basis that they are one of the 'all' group but not the 'some' one. However, using this technique should not be about lowering your expectations of what the learners can achieve; it should be about an understanding of how conceptual understanding is built gradually and an acceptance that not all learners will get to the same level of understanding of what is learnt at exactly the same time. In this instance, the learners cannot understand how to use a semicolon, unless they first understand what it can be used to separate and why it might be used in this way. This is the first step on the road to proper usage of this punctuation mark. So, your three categories could be:

- **All learners** will know what is meant by an independent clause and be able to identify one.
- **Most learners** will understand how to use a semicolon to join together two independent clauses, and have some understanding of why they might do so.
- **Some learners** will fully understand how and why semicolons are used and be able to use them spontaneously and accurately in their writing.

If you are concerned about learners 'getting away with' the minimum amount of work on the basis that they (or you) believe that they fall into the 'all' or 'most' groups, keep your differentiated learning objectives to yourself and ask all your learners to aim to be in the 'some' category by the end of the lesson.

The role of support staff

If you are working with other members of staff in your lessons, you will need to plan for what they are going to do to help you differentiate. Preferably, where time allows, you should aim to plan their input into your lesson together, so that your support staff understand what is being taught, and how best they can support the learners' learning during the lesson. The roles that support staff take in your lessons will depend on whether they are working one-to-one with an individual, for instance supporting a learner who has an EHCP (what used to be called a 'statement'), or whether they act as a general teaching assistant in lessons.

Additional members of staff can act as a really valuable resource for differentiating learning. They can:

- answer learners' questions when you are busy with someone else
- support individuals with their learning, talking them through anything they don't fully understand
- help you to ensure that individuals stay on task
- keep a check on the overall levels of focus in the room and help you identify where there are any potential problems bubbling up
- help you introduce part of the learning to the class, for instance by modelling an activity with or for you
- create displays to support learning and to aid differentiation for individuals
- help you to sort out any low-level behaviour issues, and so on.

The key to good practice when working with support staff is to prioritise good communication. This can be very tricky when there is little spare time available, but it really is essential for making the most of additional members of your teaching team. To maximise learning, support staff must fully understand the lesson content that you are going to teach. Trying to support learners in doing something that you don't actually understand yourself is nigh on impossible – in this situation support staff are more likely to add to any potential misconceptions than to help support children's learning. You may also need to get support staff on board with the whole philosophy of differentiated instruction. They need to understand the thinking behind this, how it is done, and the value of the learning that happens in this way.

Planning with support staff

If at all possible, you will want to plan with the other members of staff, and get their input and knowledge to help you understand what different learners might need. Sometimes support staff will have more knowledge about a learner than the teacher does, particularly in secondary schools, because they often spend more time working one-to-one with an individual. Your support staff may also have strengths in areas where you are weak – they could have expertise in or prior knowledge about a particular area of the curriculum, or they might be more highly skilled than you are in a particular aspect, such as technology.

Take care not to always allocate your TA, if you have one, to the lowest-attaining learners within a class, or to the groups where you find behaviour to be an issue. As the teacher, you are the person with the highest level of expertise and training in the room, and you should allocate yourself to the learners with the highest levels of need.

This is referred to as 'quality first teaching'. (An exception to this would be where the member of support staff has specialist training, for instance in an area of SEND that relates to an individual whom they support, and when they are specifically employed to work one-to-one with an individual.)

To get the best outcomes and the highest-quality differentiation, when you are planning with support staff:

- **Work together to plan specifically what they will do in the lesson:** Which groups will they be working with? What is their role in the learning? How much time will they spend on different activities?
- **Don't assume that you have to make all the decisions:** Allow your support staff to give input into the process where possible.
- **Ensure that any member of support staff understands the central concept and key objectives of the learning you are doing:** Don't assume that they understand the subject as fully as you do. It could be that you need to do a bit of teaching with your TA first, before they help you teach something to the class. This will especially be the case for secondary specialists, working in Key Stage 4, because the content is at its most complicated and not everyone will have studied all the subjects themselves when they were at school.
- **Remember that the curriculum changes over time as well:** It may also be the case that your support staff did not learn the material themselves when they were at school – for instance, the new grammatical terminology that children are expected to know in Key Stage 2, which many teachers will have had to study themselves before teaching to the children.
- **Ask your support staff for their ideas too:** This is especially important if they are working one-to-one with an individual learner in the long term.
- **Make sure you know what your support staff's plans and approaches are when they are working with individual learners:** A key part of your role is to keep a check on the progress of every member of your class, including those who have one-to-one support. Just because a TA is working with an individual, it does not mean you are no longer responsible for that learner's progress – as the class teacher, you still take overall charge.
- **Do not put your TA with the lowest-attaining group:** As the teacher, you are the most highly qualified person in the room, and you should be using your expertise to work with the learners who most need it.
- **Talk to your support staff to find out more about their areas of expertise:** Just as you need to get to know your learners, to know what learning they need to do next, so you need to get to know support staff in order to make best use of them.

The starting point for differentiation will always be about getting to know your learners better, as far as is humanly possible, so that you can plan the right kind of learning for them. Invest time in thinking lessons through ahead of time, to help you figure out the right activities to support and challenge all the learners in your class.

Chapter 2
Resources

This section looks at the wide range of resources that are available to support differentiated learning in the classroom. Resources offer an additional support that can enhance understanding or support progress for your learners. However, they do not necessarily require any teacher input to be used in a lesson. This makes them a powerful tool for differentiation – they become almost like an additional member of staff, because they can support learning without you needing to be involved. In the context of this book I use the word 'resources' to refer to all the things in the classroom, *in addition to* the teacher and the learners, that can add to or enhance the learning. As well as resources being the objects or materials that we might bring into or use in class to support learning, the classroom space itself can act as a resource for differentiation. The way we lay out our teaching space, what is on the walls, even the way that we move around inside it – all these aspects can enable progress for individual learners.

We tend to think of differentiation as being about a kind of triangle of approaches – one that happens between the teacher, the learner and the learning. However, the resources that we use will also have a significant impact on the learners and on the learning that happens in lessons. This section will help you to reflect on the ways in which you could adapt or change your teaching space in order to support differentiated teaching and learning, as well as the kind of resources you might use to support the learners within it. It is worth thinking creatively when it comes to resources – it can sometimes be the simplest of objects, combined with a great teacher explanation, that finally enables an individual to 'see' what you were getting at.

Resources offer a brilliant way to help learners to conceptualise ideas in different subjects. They help make learning hands-on and concrete, as opposed to abstract and at a distance. As well as supporting understanding, resources can help your learners generate new ideas, make learning more memorable and engaging, and show them how what you do in the classroom relates to what happens in the real world. Although there can be some classroom management issues for the teacher to think through when using resources, generally speaking they are a huge benefit for learning, and particularly for achieving differentiation in your teaching.

The teaching space

Whatever kind of differentiation strategies you use, they all take place within your teaching space or spaces. You might be teaching in a classroom, a gym, a studio, a laboratory, a hall, a playing field, a lecture theatre or maybe even a forest. But whatever space you teach in, the way you use it and the way you set it out will affect the teaching and learning that goes on inside it. Your space is one of the most important resources that you have available to use, and you make use of it every single day. Just as adapting the lesson content or approaches can help you to support learning, so adapting the space can help you to support and challenge every learner in your class as well.

Classroom layout

When we talk about classroom layout, we tend to think about how the desks are arranged – we look at the classroom from the perspective of the teacher standing at the front of it, rather than looking at the classroom from the perspective of the learners sitting at their desks or workbenches, or in a subject like PE or drama, moving around in an open space. When you think about adapting your classroom layout to support differentiation, consider how the space will impact on and feel for the learners, rather than only for you. Any adaptations you make to your space will obviously have to be very much within the realms of possibility – you may well be prevented from using your 'dream layout' simply because of the size or shape of your room. When considering how layout supports (or doesn't support) differentiation in your teaching space, consider whether your learners are able to:

- see the whiteboard or working wall areas properly
- see you clearly
- sit comfortably for the whole lesson time
- access resources easily
- share resources equitably
- avoid distractions
- come to the front if they need to access the whiteboard
- move around the space when necessary.

There is no single best layout to use, either for learning generally, or more specifically for differentiation. You might hear some people say that desks set out in rows is definitely best, or other people say that desks set out in groups is surely better. But what works best will depend on so many variables: the age of the learners, the subject being taught, the task being done, the philosophy of you as a teacher and of your school. There is no reason at all why you cannot rearrange your furniture for a lesson or for an activity (although if you share your classroom, make sure you put it back to how it was when you are done). It is well worth 'training your learners' in the efficient movement of furniture if you plan to rearrange your room frequently.

Think about how the way you have laid out your classroom might affect how much your learners participate and how they feel about learning in your lessons. How might the layout itself work against the best learning for everyone? Consider the following points:

- **Traditional arrangement of rows of desks:** In a classroom set out in a traditional arrangement of rows of desks, the learners in the centre and at the front may tend to contribute more than those at the far sides or at the back, especially because your gaze falls more easily on them. Are you inadvertently discouraging some learners from contributing because of where you sit them?
- **Think about where you as the teacher tend to look:** Are there some learners you are less likely to focus on, simply because of where they are sitting? Teachers often tend to focus on the learners who are sitting to their dominant side (i.e. the right-hand side of the room if they are right-handed). Are these the learners who most need your focus?
- **Take care not to create 'blind spots' in your classroom:** For instance, by positioning a desk where it will sometimes be obscured by a pillar, depending on where you are standing.
- **If a learner is always placed towards the back of the space:** Consider how this might subconsciously impact on their sense of how valued their input is into the lesson.
- **Think as well about the impact of the outdoor environment on your room:** A seat that is regularly baked by the sunshine in the summer may cause discomfort and distraction to a learner.

Think about how your classroom layout will impact on the learners' access to resources as well. For instance, in some lessons you might want to have stations that the learners can visit, either to access resources or to complete a particular task. If these stations are placed around the edges of the room, consider how easy it will be for the learners to cross from a desk on one side of the room to collect something from a station on the other. If you have resources on the walls – for instance, interactive vocabulary banks – think about whether it will be possible for all learners to get to these, or whether this will cause disruption to others in the room. Aim to imagine yourself as a learner within the space, and think through some 'worst case' scenarios.

Seating plans

We tend to think of seating plans as a control mechanism for behaviour, but you can also use seating plans to support differentiated learning. At the simplest level, you can use a seating plan to remind you of the differing needs in your class, by adding coded symbols or notes to your plan, for instance to remind you who are your EAL learners or who has a hearing or sight impairment. Some teachers will make a note on their class lists about whether specific learners are considered to be low or high attainers, due to their previous results in a subject, or which learners are entitled to pupil premium funding.

You can also use seating plans to support differentiation by considering where different learners sit within your classroom. A really useful exercise is to go and sit in different spots in your room, when the learners are not present. This will give you a genuine feel for how the room looks and feels from different seating positions, and give you an insight into the experience that your learners have in your lessons. Consider the specific needs of your learners, and where these might be best met within the space. For instance, you might seat a learner near the front of the room if:

- they struggle not to be distracted by the other learners
- they need regular reminders to focus during whole-class teaching
- they have a visual impairment and would benefit from being closer to the whiteboard
- they have a hearing impairment and need to be sat close to you to hear you or to see your lips moving
- they have English as an additional language and will benefit from being able to follow your face and mouth as you talk
- they are likely to need significantly more input during working tasks, and sitting at the front would make it easier for you to get to them to help
- they are a nervous individual, or they are facing a difficult situation at home, and being close to the front will allow you to give them more reassurance and support
- they are on the autistic spectrum – it may be useful to sit them towards the front in order to limit the amount of sensory input from any displays and other visuals in your room.

Take care not to get into the habit of sitting your high-attaining or very well-behaved learners with the lower-attaining ones, or those with tricky behaviour, in the expectation that they will support their partner or keep them in check behaviour-wise. While this might seem like a logical move from the perspective of the teacher, from the viewpoint of the high-attaining or well-behaved learner it can feel as though they are being punished or given a role that they didn't ask for and quite likely didn't want.

While the occasional bit of peer teaching or peer support for behaviour can work really well, doing this is not a long-term solution to a learning or behaviour issue that you have in your classroom.

The teacher within the space

Consider how you stand and move around within the space and the impact that this will have on an individual's learning, behaviour and emotions. Although you might not be aware that you are doing it, you will already differentiate your interactions with different learners according to what you know about how they will react to you. If you know that a learner is shy, you might approach them slowly and duck down below their eye level when you talk to them, to lessen any sense of threat. When you know that a learner tends to react defensively to being challenged over their behaviour, you might use non-verbal signals as opposed to verbal commands. The subtle changes that you make each and every minute of the day are all a key part of the way that you differentiate your approach to the individuals who are in your class. These tiny adaptations all help you build a relationship with your learners, which helps to enhance their learning.

Become as alert as possible about how your learners feel about how you interact with them within the space. For instance, do they sense that they are under pressure when you move closer to them, or do they feel more involved and engaged with the lesson? Consider how the eye contact you make can be a positive or a negative for different individuals – some learners will love you to look at them directly, while others will find this difficult (especially those on the autistic spectrum). It can be tempting to move around the room constantly, in order to encourage a feeling of engagement and pace. However, for some learners the teacher's movements might prove distracting. Balance times when you move and enthuse, with other times when you pause and teach from a still position. Look towards the learners as you address them. This is particularly important for any learners with a hearing impairment and for EAL learners.

Displays

Displays have a number of purposes within a teaching space. Clearly, they can add an aesthetic quality to the classroom, and they are also a great way to celebrate the learners' work by publishing it to the wider world. As well as the motivational aspects of display work though, displays can also support the learning that takes place in your classroom. Used to their best effect, displays can be part and parcel of the differentiation that goes on in your classroom. They can act as a source of information, help or challenge for learners, as required. You can use displays to support and celebrate attainment, and you can also use them to send messages about diversity and difference, the learners' individual interests and achievements, and about what is valued in your classroom.

Just as when you consider the layout of your space, it is easy to get into the habit of thinking about the displays in the room from the point of view of the adults, rather than from the point of view of the learners. Consider the different learners that you work with, and what you know from their previous reactions in the classroom. How will your displays impact on those who are easily distracted and what will they mean to the highly focused? Will your displays add to and support, or potentially distract from, the learning that happens in lessons? It can be very useful indeed, when your room is empty, to take a moment to sit in different learners' seats in various spots in the room and to view the displays from this perspective. Look around the space and consider what your learners see when you are teaching them. Ask yourself the following questions:

- What do you notice first? What attracts your attention and draws you in?
- Do the walls look very busy – is it hard to focus in on one thing?
- Would you find it hard to focus on the teacher if you were sat where your learners sit?
- Which displays remain constant and which ones have changed over time? Is there anything that has been up for more than a year?
- How many of the displays can you see from different seating positions in the room?
- Are the learners who might need to refer to a display, or who might find displays hard to see, seated near enough to them to see them?
- If there is writing on the displays, is it big enough so that you can read it from where you are sitting, or would you need to get closer to it to see it properly?
- Do the images on your displays reflect and celebrate the diversity and difference within your class, and of society generally, or do they reinforce stereotypes?
- In a class with lots of EAL learners, are there plenty of examples of writing in other languages on the walls?
- If you were planning for your learners to be able to read the writing that is on the displays, for instance to use it as a support for learning, is it big and clear enough for them to be able to do this?
- If you want the learners to interact with displays during your lessons, how easy is it going to be for them to physically gain access to them?
- If you were a learner, how easy would you find it to gather and use the information that the displays are trying to give you?

- How well do the displays in your room celebrate achievement in different areas of the curriculum? Are they broad and balanced, or focused only on the core subjects?
- What would your learners say about the displays in your classroom? How easy do they find them to use for learning? Have you ever asked them for feedback?

When you are thinking about how you could use displays to support differentiation, consider how you want your learners to use them. Think about how they will be made as well – will they be designed and created by the teacher, or will the learners be involved? Think about when in the lesson (or outside of lesson time) your learners will access the displays and how you want them to use the information they get from them. Will there be something the learners can take away from the displays to use while they are working, or are they a static source of information that stays on the wall? Will the learners be adding to and developing the displays during lessons? Are they a 'working wall' or a 'finished product'? When it comes to their uses for differentiation, your displays could be:

- a source of information and support
- a resource for inspiration and motivation
- part of the ongoing learning
- a way to stretch and challenge your learners.

Each of these is discussed below.

Displays for information and support

Some of your displays will specifically include something to support particular learners in their class work. A display might include something that learners can copy from, something to give them information to go into their work, or perhaps a framework for them to use for an activity. When you are considering displays created for information/support, it is important to ask yourself whether, if you were a learner in your class who needed to, you would be able to gather and use information from this display. If you wouldn't, then your display is more akin to wallpaper than to a differentiated source of support. Some examples of the kind of things you might put in displays made for information and support include:

- a list of key words on Velcro™, which the learners can take away to copy from while writing
- scaffolding frames for writing, for instance a scaffold that shows how to lay out a letter or a report

- examples of 'What A Good One Looks Like' (WAGOLL) in a particular part of the curriculum
- checklists for what to include in a specific piece of work
- reminders about what the learners should do when they have finished a task
- activities for the learners to do if they finish a task early.

Displays for inspiration and motivation

Seeing your work up on display is a great way to get motivated – it is like 'publishing' a learner's work to a wider audience. When you choose which examples of your learners' learning to put up on your walls, you can differentiate the messages that you want to send. For shy individuals, or those lacking in self-esteem, seeing their piece of writing, or artwork, or idea up on the wall could be a boost to confidence. For learners who tend to rush their work and make errors, the chance to have their work displayed might come in tandem with a challenge – to punctuate the piece accurately, for instance, or to correct the spellings in it before it gets displayed. Displays can also celebrate individuals who have done something 'above and beyond', and this can be a great way to boost those learners who struggle in academic subjects. Your displays designed for inspiration and motivation could include:

- images of the learners themselves being successful in a particular activity
- certificates and prizes that the learners have won doing extra-curricular activities – for instance, at a swimming gala or gymnastics competition
- fascinating objects that the learners can take away with them, to inspire their writing
- examples of inspiring adults to look up to – for instance, a snippet of J.K. Rowling's writing, or a picture of Stephen Hawking or Tanni Grey-Thompson
- a sample of each learner's 'best work', in a variety of subject areas, for instance in the form of a 'Genius wall'.

Displays for ongoing learning

One of the key issues you may face, particularly with those learners who have learning difficulties, who lack motivation, or who have difficulty with short- or long-term memory, is to get them to retain what they learnt in a previous lesson and then apply it in the next one. Displays can help a great deal with this, because they can track what happened before in your classroom, as a reminder and a refresher for learners who struggle to retain it. You can also refer to these displays during a lesson as a way to support the learners' memory of what happened.

A great technique for creating a display to support ongoing learning is to get the learners to take photographs of the learning they are doing in a lesson, at each stage of the process. You can then display these photographs in your classroom to remind them of what they did previously. This approach works particularly well for any practical tasks – the learners can look at the sequence of steps that they took when they did the task previously, to remind them of the correct approach. As well as using these photographs in a display, you could also share them on your interactive whiteboard as a refresher before doing a similar task, or as a celebration of what was achieved.

Working wall

A 'working wall' is a great example of a display that marks, celebrates and encourages ongoing learning. Working wall displays support differentiation in many different ways:

- At the start of a topic, the learners can put up questions that they would like to have answered. When you look at these questions, you will gain a sense of the different levels of knowledge and interest from which your learners are beginning their study. Are there some learners who don't seem particularly excited about this topic and, if so, how can you engage them? Are some of your learners asking particularly insightful questions and how can you stretch their thinking even further?
- At the beginning of a topic, the learners can also put up examples of the things that they already know about this subject. Again, this will give you a sense of how much prior knowledge each of your learners already has. Are there some learners who already know some of the information that you were planning to teach to the whole class? How could you utilise and build on this existing knowledge?
- The learners can add labels of different complexity to your display, as they gather information about a subject. For instance, if you had a picture of a plant on the wall, learners with weak literacy could add simple labels for each of the parts, while learners with stronger literacy skills could look up the Latin names for common plants, and add these to the display as well.
- During the topic, you could use your working wall questions as an extension task for learners who finish activities early. Can they pick a question from the wall to answer, adding their ideas to the display?
- Towards the end of the topic, you can get your learners to retrieve the questions that they posted on your working wall at the beginning, to see how they can now give answers to questions that they didn't know before. This is a great way to show them how their learning has moved forwards. Are there

any questions that you didn't manage to answer? Answering these might make a good activity for a 'flipped learning' homework.

Displays for stretch and challenge

It is not only our high-attaining learners who need to be challenged – it is our job to find the right level of stretch and challenge for every learner, by setting high expectations of what they can achieve in class. However, it is probably fair to say that it can be harder for schools to challenge those who find learning easy. If an individual reads widely and voraciously at home, or has parents who have taken them to a range of cultural activities, they are likely to find that they already know at least some of the curriculum you are planning to teach them. One way to build the thinking of learners who already know quite a bit of what you are going to cover in lessons is to challenge them via the displays in your room. You might:

- **Create a 'Genius wall' where you share examples of great work:** You could add lights or picture frames to the work on your 'Genius wall' to highlight the value that you place on it. Get the learners to think and talk about what makes these pieces of work particularly great, identifying the specific features that they feel give evidence of this. Your learners could add labels to the display to highlight these features.
- **Ask EAL learners to write captions for any posters or displays in your room in their home language:** Remember that it is easy to assume that a learner with EAL is a low attainer, when in fact it may just be the lack of language learning that is the barrier.
- **Create a 'Questions wall' where learners can post questions that they would like to explore in class:** These might be philosophical as well as academic. Your learners could also take another learner's question, and try to find an answer to it, as an extension activity in lessons.
- **Alternatively, create a 'Questions Wall' filled with examples of difficult questions that you want your learners to consider or answer on a topic:** You can also pose questions that have no right or wrong answer to get them thinking in an open-ended way.
- **Create a display of challenging texts that your learners could read:** You could display these in order of how hard they are, or give them a 'difficulty' rating out of ten. You could challenge your learners to read a book that is harder than the one they have just finished.
- **Challenge your learners to create displays themselves:** This is a great way to stretch their thinking and also to build their design and presentation skills.

Learner-created displays

In some instances, the creation of the display can become a key part of the learning process for the learners. Creating a display will challenge their creative skills, as well as encourage them to think about how much information they want to share, what format the information should be in, and how they could encourage an audience to engage with their display. Asking your learners to create a good display is a very similar challenge to asking them to do some peer teaching – they have to consider how they will get information across to a specific audience. The challenge for your learners to create their own display could form part of a lesson task, or it could act as an extension activity for those who have completed their work. For instance, your learners could create a 'how to' display of a task that they have completed in class:

- They take photographs of the various stages of a task during a lesson.
- They are challenged to sequence the photographs in the correct order to demonstrate the process.
- They create a display to show the stages of the task they did, with labels that use the language of sequencing – 'first', 'next', 'after that' and so on.
- The class as a whole can then refer back to this display if they need to, when doing a similar task in the future.

You can make learner-created displays on a small scale, just in your own classroom. However, you can also do it on a much larger scale, perhaps inviting parents and other visitors in to see the displays that your learners have created. You can see some great examples of learners acting as curators of large-scale displays on this website: **www.kidcurators.com**, where they act as curators of museum-style exhibits.

Enabling environments

The term 'enabling environments' is one that is commonly used in early years settings to describe the resources and activities that are set out for the children to play with all the time. This would include sand, water play, a book corner, a fine motor activity, and so on, and is commonly referred to as 'continuous provision'. The idea is that the environment itself is set out in such a way that it enables different children's learning across the curriculum. Differentiation comes about through the way the space is set up, and the resources that are set out within it, as well as through the teaching that is done by the adults. One of the key jobs of the practitioner or teacher is to lay out and manage the environment in such a way that the children cover the full curriculum, through a series of engaging and challenging activities.

In EYFS, and particularly in non-school settings, practitioners may be working with a wide age group within a single space. For instance, they might teach a group that includes some toddlers who are only just two, up to children who are almost five years old and who are about to start school. Because of the rapid development of children in this age group, there can be a very wide range of levels of knowledge, skills and understanding between different individuals. Some children may have no language at all yet, while others may be talking fluently. If there are children in the setting who have EAL or SEND, this adds another layer of complexity to their learning needs. In this kind of environment it would make very little sense to teach the group through lessons, as is typically done in a school.

The key resource in any EYFS setting is the practitioners themselves: it is through the way that practitioners play with, talk to and encourage the children that the children's learning develops. A high ratio of adults to children means that the adults can more easily work with individuals, and differentiate the learning for them in the moment through careful interventions. At this age, a lot of the 'stretch and challenge' will come about through the questions that the adults ask of the children and the way that they extend their thinking through discussion, talk and the use of the resources for play. Another of the key skills of an early years practitioner is to know what resources are available in their setting and to think about which ones they should use at any given moment for maximum learning. By looking at each child's 'next steps' for learning, they can decide what resources might best lead to them achieving those steps and how these resources should be set out.

It is interesting to note that this idea of self-directed learning is also being explored in other phases and in some of the more forward-thinking models for 'schools of the future' in other countries. Logically, if you want to personalise education to an individual person, you need to give each individual more control over the shape, form and timing of their own education. With the rapid development of online learning, and the growth in home education, we may well see more and more people approach their education in less conventional ways in the future, in order to maximise differentiation.

Planning boards

Planning boards are a good way to ensure that children in EYFS access all the different areas during continuous provision time, and that you don't end up with a big crowd of children in one place, and none in another. This strategy is especially useful when you have a large group of children, or a mixed-age class of EYFS/Key Stage 1 learners, in which some of the children will be playing while you do whole class teaching with the others. Planning boards also encourage a sense of personal responsibility, because they ask the children to take control of planning their own learning. To use planning boards in EYFS:

- Take a picture of each area of your continuous provision and put these up on the wall somewhere easily accessible.
- Stick Velcro™ pads around the outside of the picture – stick the number of pads that represent how many children you feel should use this area as a maximum at any one time.
- Now create a Velcro™ name label for each child.
- If the children can write their names, they could do this themselves; if they might not recognise their own names then you could use a symbol instead.
- Explain to the children that, before they go to play in a particular area of the provision, they need to take their name and stick it beside the related picture.
- If all the pads are full, they should choose another area to play in for the time being.
- In a busy setting with lots of children, you could add a time limit to specify how long anyone can spend in each area.
- You could also keep a note of where the children play, to ensure curriculum coverage.

To use planning boards to differentiate further, you could:

- Ask a particular child to make sure that they play in a specific area. This could be an area they would not gravitate to of their own accord, but where there is a gap in their learning.
- Make a note of which children spend time in which areas, adapting what is in each area to ensure that they get full coverage of the curriculum. For instance, you can add numbers to the sand if a child always plays there, if you are concerned that the child tends not to access numeracy resources independently.
- Set targets for individual children about how many areas they will visit during the course of a session.
- Create an incentive for children to play in each area – for instance, picking up a piece of 'treasure' in each different part of your provision.

Using learners' interests as a resource

Practitioners in the early years are highly attuned to their children's interests. This is a non-statutory phase of a child's education, and many young children will be in an early years setting for far longer hours than they will ever be in school. It is therefore only right and respectful that we incorporate their interests into our provision. Using a child's interests also acts as a way to motivate children, and to encourage them to learn in all areas of the curriculum, because you can draw them into specific areas of your provision through the way you resource it. As our learners get older, we tend to see their interests as a potentially limiting factor – how will we get them to learn about things they don't have an interest in if we focus on what they already like? However, this underestimates the importance of personal motivation in the effort required to make progress, and it ignores the fact that you can easily use their interests as a 'hook' for new learning.

For instance, if an individual has shown a great interest in dinosaurs, an early years practitioner might:

- put dinosaur books into the reading area
- create a dinosaur small world on a tuff tray
- set up a trail of dinosaurs that leads outdoors
- get the children to dip dinosaur feet in paint in the art corner
- hide dinosaur cards in the sand pit.

As well as being a very useful technique in EYFS, using learners' interests is a great way to support differentiation for different age groups, because it encourages an engagement with and a focus on learning. We tend to concentrate more on the core curriculum, and less on each learner's personal interests, as the learners get older. However, it is still possible to allude to, incorporate and combine personal interests with the wider curriculum. This is perhaps especially important if you work with youngsters who struggle to see the relevance of school.

For example, if a young person has demonstrated a strong interest in music, you could:

- use song lyrics as an example of poetry, to engage them with English lessons
- use music as the basis for a study of the science of sound
- offer the chance to listen to music as a reward for hard work in a lesson
- use music as the basis for a design technology project, in which the learners devise a stand for a music player.

Methods for differentiation by resource

The resources you use to differentiate and to support understanding can make a huge difference to the learning experience that learners have in your classroom. Getting hands-on with a resource can really bring a subject to life for a learner, and it could illuminate a tricky concept as well. Think laterally about what an individual or class might need in order to better understand a subject, to differentiate the task or goal, or to help you check and assess what they are learning. Useful resources come in all shapes and sizes, and a single resource can be used in a whole host of different ways. A resource designed for one subject (e.g. cuisenaire rods in maths) can often be used in another way in a different subject (for instance, using the rods to make patterns in art). The skill of seeing how a resource could be adapted and used flexibly to support differentiated learning is a key attribute of the effective educator.

Resources basically fall into two categories:

- resources that are created or designed specifically for teaching and learning purposes – numicon, writing frames, educational apps, and so on
- resources that we pick up or gather from our lives outside the classroom, and which we might use imaginatively and inventively to motivate a learner or to bring a concept to life.

One of the most powerful moments as a teacher is when you spot a resource that you know will help an individual learner understand an idea or a concept. This is differentiation in action.

Resources can be used for several different purposes:

- resources for support
- resources for challenge
- resources for checking understanding
- resources for motivation and focus
- resources for supporting writing.

Each of these different approaches is discussed below.

Resources for support

Some of the resources that you use will be specifically designed to support the understanding and learning of individual learners or groups of learners. A resource for support will often tend to be a simplified version of what is available to everyone else, something that explains the learning in a different, more accessible way, or something that removes a barrier that might otherwise be in place. As well as using such resources to support your learners in the classroom, you can also offer resources that will help your learners and their families at home.

For instance, you might:

- with younger children, put a picture that starts with the same letter as the child's name alongside their coat peg, to support them in recognising the name/picture combination
- add translations of signs into the first languages of the learners and families using your setting
- have a sign saying 'hello' or 'welcome' in a range of community languages
- put up a display for parents, giving ideas to support their child's learning at home
- offer leaflets about supporting early reading, or how to help with homework, in different community languages
- record your explanation of an activity, so that the learner can listen to it several times over
- offer learners a translated version of a text to read at home, before you study it in class
- allow learners who struggle to write notes to use a recording device to gather their ideas.

Resources for challenge

The kind of resources that challenge your learners will often be the ones that push them to do more open-ended or abstract thinking, or that require them to use higher-order thinking skills, such as analysis or evaluation. Remember that challenge is not just about the learner doing more of the same, it is about creating opportunities for deeper or wider types of learning. For instance, you could:

- offer your learners a resource that creates opportunities for open-ended and higher-order thinking, such as a pile of large, empty cardboard boxes
- use resources to create a 'provocation' – a scenario in which the learners are challenged to solve a problem, come up with a solution or work out a puzzle
- ask the learners to find resources to create a provocation or puzzle of their own, with which to challenge you or their classmates
- have a 'challenge box' available as an extension activity, with questions, challenges and puzzles written on slips of paper inside.

Resources for understanding

While some learners find it reasonably easy to grasp complex abstract concepts, others really benefit from a concrete demonstration in order to understand an idea. This can vary according to the subject – some learners may find mathematical concepts easy to grasp, but struggle with conceptualising ideas in literacy, and vice versa. Think about how you can use objects, demonstrations, stories and examples to teach a concept and to support learning for all your learners. This will also help you enliven your lessons and better engage your classes. As well as working well with a whole class, these resources can also be very helpful for individuals. Getting hands-on with an object can help make a concept more memorable for a learner, as well as making it easier for them to understand. Some learners may need you to talk them through several different concrete examples before they grasp a new concept.

The best concrete examples will typically:

- relate to something that the learners already know about
- have a direct relationship to 'real life'
- involve an interesting object to help make an idea memorable
- link to something that the learners are already interested in
- involve telling a story or sharing an anecdote
- get the learners active and involved in their learning.

For instance, a maths teacher once used a concrete example to help me understand how to add and subtract negative numbers, using ice cubes and a baby bath:

- the ice cubes stand for negative numbers
- the bath stands for zero (or whatever number you want to begin with)
- as you 'add' ice cubes to the bath, the temperature goes down
- as you 'subtract' ice cubes from the bath, the temperature goes up
- in the same way, as you 'add' negative numbers, the number goes down, and as you 'subtract' them, the number goes up.

Another excellent resource to support understanding is the 'graphics organiser', which combines text and images to explain information. You can find out more about this idea in Chapter 4 (page 93).

Resources for checking understanding

One of the key pieces of information you need in order to be able to differentiate effectively is whether or not your learners have understood something that you have just explained to them. Resources can be very useful in helping you to gauge the level of understanding across a group, and of individual learners. You can use resources to check for understanding at the start of a lesson or during the course of it. You can also use them to see how well you got a subject across to your learners, and what teaching you might still need to do on it, after the lesson has finished.

For instance, you could use:

- **Mini whiteboards:** These can help you check whether your learners have understood. Ask them to complete an example on their whiteboards and to show you their answers. How many of them have got it right? Which individuals don't seem to understand and might benefit from further instruction?
- **An indicator:** Use an indicator to check how many learners can confirm that they are clear about what you taught, and how many need further input. You could use green/amber/red cards, or a thumbs up or down system, to divide the class into 'yes I get it', 'I'm not one hundred per cent sure' and 'no, I don't understand this at all'. (Bear in mind that if you use this technique, you need to be sure that your learners will be confident enough to be honest with you.)
- **An electronic voting, survey or response system:** Ask some multiple choice questions. The responses you get will help you gauge who has understood a particular aspect of the curriculum.
- **A 'corkboard'-style online tool such as padlet.com:** Everyone can contribute their thoughts, ideas or answers in a single shared space.
- **A set of prompts that get learners to evaluate their own understanding and learning:** For instance, what are your strengths and weaknesses in this area? How easy or difficult did you find this?
- **A '3-2-1' format:** Ask the learners to list three things they found out during the lesson, two things they found interesting, and one thing they still don't understand or would like to know more about.
- **Progress checklists:** You can complete these over the course of a unit of learning. Your checklist could include 'can do' statements, with varying levels of complexity. For instance, in English your statements about punctuation could be: (a) can use full stops accurately; (b) can use commas correctly in a list; (c) can use semicolons correctly.
- **Exit tickets:** These are completed at the end of a session, to see how fully your learners have understood the content. Your exit tickets could be done online, for example using Google Forms, or you could use a written exit ticket, for instance with a question on it that tests for understanding.

Resources for motivation and focus

One of the key aspects missing from their education for some of our learners is a sense of motivation and focus. Without these two attributes, progress can be slow. There are lots of resources that the teacher can utilise to improve motivation and focus. For instance, it is always useful to have a time limit and a target for an activity, because it focuses the mind wonderfully. If a learner is given 'three minutes to come up with as many ideas as you can' or 'five minutes to complete ten questions' this encourages them to work fast and to focus on the end goal. Resources are a fantastic way to make these time limits and targets clear and concrete for your learners. There are many options available to the teacher, to use both with a whole class and also with individuals – large sand timers, timers on your electronic whiteboard, individual stopwatches, and so on.

While time limits and targets are a useful strategy to motivate a whole class, they can also be incorporated at an individual or group level, to support differentiation for the learners who really need a focus. A target or a time limit can work as a challenge to high-attaining or well-motivated learners, as well as an encouragement to lower-attaining or less-focused ones. Some learners will struggle to stay on task, either because they find it hard to focus or because they are poorly motivated to do so. For these learners, you can incorporate resources to help them maintain concentration.

You might:

- use an individual timer for a learner who needs reassurance – turning it over and letting them know that you will come back to see how they are doing, before the time is up
- use an individual timer to give a learner a specific target – can they complete x number of questions before the sand runs through?
- ask the learner to put the timer on its side if they get stuck, to give you an indication that they need some support.

Give regular reminders of time left to the whole class – a timer on your electronic whiteboard can help them understand how much time is remaining. Remember too that your 'time given' does not have to be accurate. You can 'cheat' the time a bit, extending it if the learners look really focused or cutting it down if you sense that they have already almost finished, or are losing focus. You might ask a learner who has finished early to take over the timing for you, as an added challenge.

Another good way to set motivational targets for individuals is to keep a highlighter handy. As you move around the classroom you could highlight:

- the section of a worksheet or text that you want a learner to focus on next
- the parts of the work that need proofreading and/or correcting
- the bits of the work that are particularly good, and that you'd like to see more of.

Resources for supporting writing

Resources to support writing tend to offer learners a 'halfway house' to a piece of writing that is done completely independently. When you create a framework or a scaffold to support writing, you want to give the learners enough support to be able to complete the task, or to do it well, but not so much that you effectively do the activity for them. These scaffolds can range in the amount of support they offer. You could allow all or most of your learners to use whatever scaffold you offer, or you could encourage some of them to work independently from the word go. Some learners will need a great deal of propping up with scaffolds, because of SEND or perhaps EAL, but there is a distinct danger of an over-reliance on frameworks, and in turn a sense of learnt helplessness. Remove the scaffolds as soon as possible, and if the learners can manage without them, then encourage them to do so.

Some of the resources you use to support writing might include:

- **Cloze procedure pieces:** Where the learner only has to fill in a few gaps in a piece of writing, and is perhaps even given the vocabulary with which to do so.
- **Writing frames or frameworks:** Where the main structure is given to the learner, for instance the outline of a letter.
- **Sentence starters:** The opening for a sentence, perhaps written on a lollipop stick or on a structure strip that learners can stick down the side of a page in their books to help them structure their writing.
- **Individual word cards:** Where you give the learner a few words that you want them to incorporate into their writing, perhaps as a challenge.

Writing overlays

Writing overlays offer a way to add information or support to a piece of learning, particularly if you are working with learners who have significant SEND. This approach helps the learners learn how to find information from a picture. Here's how it works:

- Create a laminated overlay with a gap in the middle.
- Put a series of questions around the edges of the overlay frame, related to the subject you are studying, in a clockwise direction.
- Each question should build in complexity or difficulty on the one before it. For instance, the first question might be simply to identify something in the picture, whereas later ones could be about making inferences and deductions.

- Now overlay your frame on a picture.
- The learners should work their way around the frame, in a clockwise direction.
- As they move around the frame they answer each question directly onto the laminate, referring back to the picture in the centre for information to use in their answers.
- The answers can be transferred into a book or photographed, then you can wipe clean the frame and start over again with a different picture.
- You could also add a set of key words to the frame, and ask that the learners tick each one off as they use it.

For instance, if your focus was on the study of different texts in English literature, you could put a still from the film of the text in the centre, and then use the following questions on your overlay frame:

- What characters from the story can you see in this image?
- What do you think the characters are doing in the picture?
- Which part of the story do you think this image is from?
- Why do you think this image is from that part of the story?
- Can you write down a quote from this part of the story?
- How does this quote relate to some of the themes in the story?

Technological resources

We live in a time when there has been an explosion in the forms of technology that are available, and in some ways we are still working through the impact that this will have on our classrooms. Technology can allow us to support and extend learning, and it can also help us take learning outside the classroom, linking up to learners, educators and schools right around the world. We have a huge amount of information at our fingertips, as do our learners. Navigating our way through the many technological advances is probably one of the biggest challenges in education at the start of the 21st century.

Technology can be a great equaliser for learners with different needs. The pace of change in technology over the last 20 years has been astonishing. There are so many options that will now allow you to differentiate for learning, particularly for learners who have SEND. For severely disabled learners, there are now technologies available such as eye gaze frames that allow an individual to point with their eyes. Learners with severe literacy difficulties can use voice recognition software to express their ideas. There really are a huge number of ways in which technology can help you differentiate learning to the individuals within your class.

You might:

- create folders of articles that you think particular learners might like to read, and put these into a shared online space
- create a class blog, on which learners can write about what they have learnt in class that day
- give your learners access to materials online, ahead of lessons, to support their understanding in class
- use an interactive assessment tool, such as **socrative.com**, to check where your learners are with their learning during the lesson, or at the end of it
- create videos that you want the learners to watch ahead of the lesson, or edit existing videos by adding voice-overs, etc
- use interactive maths websites that allow learners to progress at their own pace, such as **mymaths.co.uk**
- use a tool such as **rewordify.com** to simplify texts and make them more accessible for your learners
- offer recording devices as an alternative to handwriting
- use online timers on your interactive whiteboard
- utilise QR codes to share examples of your learners' work with their parents
- ask learners to watch a YouTube video prior to a lesson, to support their understanding when you teach them.

Assistive technology

There is a wide range of assistive technology that is now available to support learning, particularly for those learners who have SEND. This technology can offer help for the most severely disabled – for instance, eye-tracker software to allow an individual with no speech to communicate. It can also give help to those learners who need a more minimal form of support – for example, spellcheckers. Just as with the use of writing scaffolds, as an educator you will need to strike a balance between offering your learners enough support to learn successfully, and giving them so much support that they become over-reliant on it, and never learn to do the work for themselves. This is something that should be decided on a case-by-case basis – there is no such thing as the right answer for all.

Here are some examples from SEND specialist Jules Daulby of assistive technology that you might find especially useful:

- software that reads text from a screen, such as *Clicker*, *Claro* or *Read&Write Gold*

- voice recognition software, for example *Dragon NaturallySpeaking* or the built-in software that comes with Windows
- concept mapping software, for instance *Inspiration* or *Popplet*
- built-in accessibility features, such as read view in Word, or making changes to the text size, font used, and so on
- organisational software – choose from a variety of online timetables and calendars that give reminders
- using photos for various purposes, for instance taking pictures of homework.

Managing resources within the space

It is often the case that those learners who have the most difficulty in learning need to access resources to support them most frequently. They might need to use a hands-on resource like numicon or cuisenaire rods to support maths learning; they might need to look up a word in a dictionary or use a word card to check a spelling. When you think about differentiation in the context of classroom layout, it makes sense to ensure that these learners can easily get to the places where the resources are stored. Bear in mind too that learners who have EAL, or who are not yet reading, might need support in figuring out which resources go where. Add images or translations to the drawers or other places where you store your resources.

You could create a 'resource station' that your learners can visit when they need additional support, to gather a variety of resources to take back to their desks, or to take home with them to support homework. Alternatively you might have a set of resources in a container that can be placed on the tables of the learners who need them. The resources you have in your station or container will obviously vary according to the age of the learners. In a secondary classroom you might have two resource stations: one for learners in Key Stage 3 and another for those in Key Stage 4. Your resource stations might include some or all of the following resources:

- literacy mats (laminated mats with key terminology on them)
- topic mats (with key words for a topic)
- reference books such as dictionaries and thesauruses
- past papers from GCSEs for learners who are about to sit their exams
- sample exam questions
- sample essay plans
- sample exam answers
- sample mark schemes
- information sheets
- sentence starters (these can go on lollipop sticks).

Resources offer a brilliant way to support learning in the classroom and to challenge your learners to develop their thinking further. Think creatively about the resources you use, and how you use them, to help you differentiate as fully as possible in your lessons.

Chapter 3
The learners

This chapter looks at differentiation from the point of view of the learners. How do we find out what our learners already know and can do, and how do we build on this? How can we be sure that we are stretching all our learners, as well as supporting them, as and when they need? What do our attempts at differentiation say about our attitudes towards them? Occasionally, individuals will complain that it is 'not fair' when another learner gets more support than they do. (Perhaps we have partially trained them into this mindset, through our use of competitive activities in schools.) It is important to help your learners understand the thinking behind the differentiation you do, so make sure that you talk to them about it. Explain to them that being 'fair' does not necessarily mean everyone getting the same thing; instead it means giving everyone the support they need to succeed.

You can help your learners to understand what you mean by using the example of someone who needs to use a wheelchair to get around, because they cannot walk. No one would have a problem with that learner using a wheelchair to access and get around a school – we wouldn't insist that they get up and walk, because they can't. In exactly the same way, an individual may need to be given additional support or help in class to help them access the learning. When the 'disability' is not a physical one, it might be less obvious that the help is needed, because we cannot see it, but the support still has the same positive effect. Even the youngest children can understand these concepts – in fact, the younger they are, often the better they are at being truly inclusive.

When thinking about our learners, and how best to support them, we need to acknowledge that we are affected by our own perceptions of them. For instance, it can be hard to gauge how much effort our learners are putting into their work. This can lead to us thinking that some learners need to be more motivated or work harder, when what they actually need is more support. Do some learners genuinely struggle with learning, or are they just being careless with their approach? Are they really being lazy, or do they really not understand? The judgements we make about these questions can affect our entire approach to individual learners. To an extent, you will only really be able to tell, or get close to figuring this out, once you get to know your learners really well. Learners with difficulties will often hide them behind a brave front, or attempt to mask them with challenging behaviour. Remember that you can differentiate for levels of motivation, as well as for levels of attainment. While the reason behind the lack of progress might be about motivation rather than about ability, our response can still be to try to personalise our approach to the individual.

Even though we might assume that most of a learner's learning goes on at school, in fact, as the original EYFS guidance pointed out, 'parents are children's first and most enduring educators' (QCA, 2000, p. 9). Building a strong home–school relationship is crucial in helping us to understand what each of our learners needs to support their learning, and how best we can stretch them as well. Even if you are a primary teacher who spends an entire year seeing the children all day every day, the people who know their children best are still their parents. Turning to parents for help and support is a key way to challenge and get the best out of every learner.

Learner profiles

As a starting point for getting to know more about your learners, it is useful to set them a short activity at the start of the year in which they give you a bit more information about themselves. Depending on their age and the subject you are teaching, this might mean asking their parents for the information, it could be a talk-based activity that you do together, or it might be a written one. Your learner profiles can be structured in a variety of ways. You might, for example, ask the learners to create:

- a letter from them to you, about their attitudes to learning in general, and what they enjoy and don't enjoy about school
- a letter about how they feel towards the subject you will be teaching them, if you are working in secondary education
- a short summary of their likes/dislikes, areas of interest, subject strengths and concerns, and so on
- a 'Top trumps'-style card, telling you about their super powers and their weaknesses
- a 'show me five' activity, in which the learners give you five answers in different categories – their five favourite animals, their five favourite TV shows, and so on
- a questionnaire designed to find out as much about the learners as you can
- as a slightly more unusual alternative, I once asked a class to write their own obituaries, telling me about all the exciting things they had done during their lives.

You might prefer to use an 'All about me' sheet, with prompts asking questions about various different areas of the learners' lives. This could include their interests, their family background, their favourite subjects, their areas of strength and weakness, and so on. You can find some nicely illustrated examples for doing this task online. Younger children could fill out an 'All about me' sheet with the help of parents, or parents could fill it out for them, when they start at your setting.

As well as it being useful to create a learner profile at the start of the school year, you can also use it as a useful pre-transition activity. The learners could be asked to write to someone at their next setting, for instance their new head teacher, about their hopes, expectations and aspirations for their new school. For these to prove useful, you will need to make time to read and respond to them – giving learners a sense of agency and ownership in their learning is only helpful when they feel that you actually listen to what they say.

Personality

In part, the way that you differentiate as an educator is as much about your personality, and those of your learners, as it is about knowledge or skills. It is a truism to say that we each have our own personality, but it would be hard not to agree that some of us are extroverts, some of us are introverts, some of us are highly conscientious perfectionists, and others of us are willing to give anything a go, no matter how messy the outcome. All of these personality traits will impact on our learning in a classroom situation, and so it is important to understand how this might affect your learners' learning, and also your teaching. A higher degree of self-awareness is never a bad thing to have.

Often, the strategies you use to cater for different personalities will be subtle and perhaps subconscious – ones that an observer might not spot or ones that you yourself might not even be aware of using. And yet these strategies are the ones that help you build the strongest kinds of relationships with your learners. If you are being observed, and your observer questions you about differentiation, it is worth reflecting on and identifying the choices that you made during the lesson because of your understanding of the individuals in your class. For example, by saying: 'Well of course, I did x because I know y about z', you will demonstrate that you reflect on and are conscious about the methods that you use to differentiate.

When you differentiate to take personality into account, this might mean that you:

- understand that a learner lacks in confidence, and that it is therefore important not to put them on the spot
- know when to draw out a quiet learner, in order to boost their confidence
- sense when some of the quieter learners in the class need some calm time, and ask that everyone works silently for a while

- know when to pick a shy learner to answer a question to increase their self-esteem, because you have the suspicion that they will get this particular question right
- understand when to ignore a loud and confident learner, to encourage them to control their own noise levels
- see when to intervene quickly to stop individuals' behaviour, and when your best bet is to completely ignore it.

Relationships

All teaching takes place within a relationship, usually between a teacher and a learner although sometimes from learner to learner as well. The way that you build up a relationship with the learners you teach will affect the quality of the differentiation that takes place in your lessons. This is not to say that you have to be liked to teach well, and for your learners to learn well, but it certainly helps to have at least some form of bond or connection with the people you are teaching. Consider how your learners feel when they come into your teaching space. It is all too easy to forget that they have an *emotional* reaction to being in the school and your classroom, as well as an *intellectual* one. Perhaps the learners are thinking:

- Will I be accepted here?
- Is this subject/lesson going to be too hard for me?
- Will I be able to keep up with the other learners?
- How can I make a contribution to this class?
- How can I be me in these lessons?
- How much ownership of or input into my learning will I have with this teacher?
- How tense or relaxed will I feel in this environment?
- Will I understand what people want from me – the adults and my peers?
- Will I get enough support/time to be able to do the work?
- What's the point in me being here?
- Does this learning seem worthwhile?
- Should I persist with this learning?
- What happens if I don't persist, if I find this too hard, or if I don't complete the work in the time that I'm given?

It is important to try to figure out how the learners are actually experiencing what and how you are teaching them. Not how you imagine they are experiencing it, but what they are actually getting from it and feeling about it. When you can create an open climate, in which honesty is valued and different opinions are accepted and respected, then you will be in a better position for your learners to open up to you. It can be really hard to be self-reflective about this – to open up to the possibility that our learners might not experience our lessons as we imagine they do. Building a sense of empathy with your learners is hard but very worthwhile.

Prior learning

As we have seen in Chapter 1, differentiation is not necessarily about giving out different activities to your learners for them to complete, it is about figuring out where they are in their learning at that moment, and then deciding how to build on that. Often, you won't be able to personalise this to any great extent, especially in a secondary school, where the demands of the curriculum, and of one teacher giving one lesson to lots of different groups of 30 or more learners, make the task too enormous to personalise the learning very much. However, if you know for sure that a learner already knows and is secure in something that you are going to be teaching, there is little point in teaching it to them all over again.

As a parent, I have experienced my own children's frustration with this issue. As avid readers, they both have a fairly wide knowledge of topics that are of interest to them, and when these topics are covered in school they are basically being taught something they already know. Despite the best efforts of teachers, it can be very hard to stretch learners who have a great deal of prior learning, at the same time as supporting those who struggle to learn. A good example of this would be the individual who has already read the book you are reading in class. It can be a huge challenge to our thinking to accept that our carefully-planned lesson might be a waste of time for some of our learners. To differentiate for learners who have a lot of prior learning in a topic, you could:

- ask them to prepare and present part of the lesson
- allow them to play an alternative role in the lesson, for instance acting as a 'spotter' to identify good work or doing some small-group teaching
- move them to a different class for a period of time, just as you might withdraw a learner for an intervention
- give them a different task to the rest of the class, one that can be done independently.

Classroom and behaviour management

It is useful to note that differentiation can be about the approaches to behaviour and classroom management issues in your classroom, as well as the way that you plan for learning. Just as with their learning, individuals respond in differing ways to different kinds of structures, motivators and consequences. This is not to say that you differentiate the rules you have in place in your classroom – your learners need to know where they stand. However, you can be flexible in the way that you deal with individuals, without this meaning that you have different expectations of them or that you lower the standards for some. Consistency of standards is important, but that does not mean that we have to use the same methods to get to those standards for every learner. Flexibility means differentiating your ways of getting to those same expectations, rather than differentiating the expectations themselves. For instance, for the same infringement (e.g. not wearing a tie) you might use the following strategies with different learners, depending on your understanding of how they would react:

- **A quick glance, a raised eyebrow and a gesture:** To learners who know the rules, who will be clear about what the problem is, and who understand non-verbal communication easily.
- **A quiet word in their ear:** For learners who tend to forget what the rule is, who often need a reminder and who respond well to one-to-one verbal communications.
- **Saying 'I'd love to give you a positive comment today – let's see if you can show me a smart and correct uniform':** To learners who are disaffected, but who respond well to rewards and praise.
- **A comment to the whole class that 'I'm looking to see who is wearing their tie really smartly':** If you know that an individual comment is likely to set a particular learner off.
- **A decision to get the class on-task first, and to deal with the issue of the missing tie privately a bit later on in the lesson:** If you know that a particular learner is likely to kick off the minute you talk to them about it.
- **A very quiet word:** With a learner who you know has a very difficult home situation, perhaps offering to loan them a tie or advising where they can get hold of a spare one.

Motivation and rewards

Motivation is a highly complex area of human behaviour – what motivates one person will not be the same as what motivates another. A 'one-size-fits-all' policy is probably as inappropriate for motivation as it is for learning. Teachers tend to use both rewards and sanctions to try to motivate their learners to behave as they want them to, usually with a focus on the use of positive approaches first, and punitive measures as a last resort. Schools will often have a single system of rewards and consequences that they wish staff to apply consistently. Typically, the system will 'work' for the majority, in that it will get them doing what you want them to. However, there will be some outliers for whom, no matter how many rewards or punishments you give, they make little difference to their behaviour or to their attitude towards learning. Just as we need to differentiate in order to get to the best learning outcomes for all our learners, so we might also need to accept that we should differentiate in order to ensure that all our learners feel motivated to engage, to work hard and to learn.

Some learners appear to have an intrinsic desire to work hard and behave well. These are the 'always' learners – the ones who always focus, always listen, always turn up on time and always work their hardest. These learners tend to get on very well in a school situation – the teachers like them and they get plenty of positive feedback and are academically successful. Often, these learners will have come from a supportive home background and will generally find learning fairly easy. Interestingly, not only are extrinsic rewards often unnecessary for these learners, they can also be counter-productive. The learners might start to believe that the reason they should work hard is connected to the kind of specific rewards they receive for that, rather than for the intrinsic joy of learning.

On the other hand, there are some learners who do not seem to be so intrinsically motivated to learn and behave in school. Perhaps their experiences of learning to date have put them off it; maybe they need more of a structured approach to motivation; perhaps something about their home life has left them disengaged with learning. For these learners, extrinsic motivators such as stickers and certificates can sometimes be the trick to increase motivation. The skill is in the teacher knowing when to trust the intrinsic motivation to do the trick, and when to give an external reward. Teachers often feel like they are giving lots of rewards to their most difficult or lowest-attaining learners and giving relatively few to the easier ones. It is worth having this conversation with your class – letting them know that you appreciate that some or many of them 'just do it', but that you understand that some of them need more support to stay focused and motivated.

While consequences need to be pretty clear-cut – behaviour x leads to consequence y – there can be a bit more leeway over the type of rewards you use. When it comes to rewards, a 'one-size-fits-all' system can only motivate those learners who respond well to the reward in question. Or, to put it another way, if I don't want the sticker you give me, then the sticker will not act as a motivator for me. You can personalise the rewards to the learners that you actually work with, rather than (or as well as) using your school system. As well as differentiating between the rewards you use with individuals, if you teach at secondary level, you might choose to differentiate between the rewards you use with different year groups or classes.

Your differentiated rewards might involve:

- a phone call home for learners who are really keen to please their parents
- a volunteer task for a learner who loves to be given jobs to do

- a chance to show work to the head of year for a learner who you know gets on well with that person
- the opportunity to receive a certificate in assembly for learners who love public acclamation
- the chance to watch a short YouTube clip at the end of a lesson for the class who told you that this would make them work harder.

When you are giving rewards, it can work very well to ask your learners what they actually want, as opposed to making assumptions. They will often come up with ideas that might surprise you, or that you might not have thought of. For instance, a teacher once told me that her class loved the chance to watch clips of *Man versus food* (a YouTube video series) at the end of lessons, as a reward for getting all their work done.

Learners with SEND

We might assume that all differentiation is about learners who have some form of SEND, but in fact differentiation goes much further than that – it extends to our relationship with each and every learner. Although it is not usually possible to differentiate for every learner in a class as far as we might like, it is still a noble aim. However, it is clear that differentiation is of the utmost importance for those learners who have SEND. The designation of SEND denotes that the learners need something 'special' in order to be able to access the curriculum in the same way that other learners might do. Two very useful guides to thinking about inclusion and differentiation for learners with SEND are: *Inclusion for Primary School Teachers* (Gedge, 2016) and *Bloomsbury CPD Library: Supporting Children with Special Educational Needs and Disabilities* (Drabble, 2016).

Learners who have SEND may be entitled to special access arrangements and reasonable adjustments when taking public examinations. Speak to your school's SENDCo for more information, and visit the JCQ's (Joint Council for Qualifications) website (**jcq.org.uk**) for the most up-to-date advice.

Types of SEND

There are a range of types of SEND that you might encounter in your career as a teacher. Bear in mind that, just because a learner does not have an EHCP, this does not mean that they do not have any special needs at all. It is perfectly possible for SEND to remain undiagnosed during a learner's school career, and for a diagnosis of, say, dyslexia or autism to only be given later on in life. It is also the case that you can and should deal with the needs of the learners in front of you even if an individual was never to get a diagnosis of SEND at all. If you sense that a learner does have a problem that has not been identified, then you should speak to your SENDCo. Do not assume that someone else will always deal with or pick up on the issue.

The terminology used around SEND changes constantly, and so do the categories of need. At the time of writing, the four main categories of SEND are classified as:

- cognition and learning
- communication and interaction
- sensory and physical
- social, emotional and mental health.

Within these categories, you might come across learners with various needs. Learners may well have needs that fall into more than one of the categories. Some of the conditions that you might come across will include:

- **Communication and language difficulties:** Such as dyslexia or a phonological processing disorder.
- **Autistic spectrum conditions:** These are on a spectrum that includes a range of levels of need.
- **Problems specific to an area of the curriculum, or to a skill set:** Such as dyscalculia, dyspraxia or dysgraphia.
- **Hearing, sight and other physical impairments.**
- **Difficulties that present at least partly as behavioural issues:** Such as ADHD (attention deficit hyperactivity disorder).

Building your knowledge about particular areas of SEND will help you to figure out the right way to differentiate for your learners. Where an individual has been assessed and has an EHCP, this document will give you lots of information on the learner's difficulties and on the strategies that you need to use. Bear in mind that some of the strategies that work well for the majority of your learners might not be appropriate for an individual with a specific learning difficulty. You may need to adjust your normal strategies and approaches to be fully inclusive. Below you can find some ideas for differentiation when working with learners on the autistic spectrum, or with working memory problems, dyslexia or ADHD.

As well as building your knowledge about SEND, you can also learn strategies that, while originally designed to support learners with special needs, are also just as useful for those without. For instance, in many early years settings, children are now taught to use Makaton (a type of sign language). Originally devised by speech and language therapists who were working with deaf children, by teaching Makaton more widely in settings, everyone can benefit from an inclusive approach. Visit **makaton.org** to find out more.

Learners on the autistic spectrum

Learners who are on the autistic spectrum will need you to differentiate your techniques specifically for them. What works well for most learners might be counterproductive for learners on the autistic spectrum. Much will depend on where the learners are on the autistic spectrum. One of the main messages from those who have expertise in working with learners on the autistic spectrum is the importance of routines. You should avoid sudden or unexpected changes, because individuals will find it particularly difficult to cope with these. You may be able to capitalise on their visual and spatial strengths – for instance, demonstrating how to put their book bag in the right place, to help them remember where it goes. When giving explanations and instructions, aim to be as specific as possible – learners on the autistic spectrum take people literally, so avoid using colloquialisms and idioms. Aim not to be too open-ended – again, learners will tend to take you literally.

It is a good idea to create a visual schedule of your school day for learners on the autistic spectrum, as this has a number of benefits:

- It supports their understanding of classroom routines.
- It helps to support their sequential memory and their understanding of time.
- It helps them develop organisational skills.
- It lessens anxiety, by showing them when changes will happen.
- It helps to support them in becoming increasingly independent.
- It can also help them to incorporate social interactions into their day.

Consider developing the visual schedule in conjunction with each individual learner, rather than presenting them with one that you have already made. Bear in mind that, for learners on the autistic spectrum, a visual schedule must be explicitly taught and consistently used. Do not see it as a crutch to wean them off, in the same way that you might wean learners off a writing scaffold to get them to learn independently. To make a visual schedule work to its full potential:

- use a top-to-bottom or a left-to-right format, and keep this consistent
- encourage the learner to cross off the routines as they are doing them (if you laminate the schedule, these can be rubbed off so that you can start again each day)
- pair written instructions with visual symbols to support the learner's understanding of what each one means
- a learner might find it useful to have a card to take with them during a transition – for instance, taking a card with them that tells them that they are to go to the assembly hall now
- 'first/then' cards can also be useful – a card that explains 'First you do x, then you do y'.

In terms of teaching strategies for learners on the autistic spectrum, the following strategies are considered to be best practice:

- Offer headphones or earplugs to wear, to limit unwanted sensory inputs if they wish, particularly in noisy environments.
- Flag up any changes to the daily routine before they happen.
- Avoid using colloquialisms, because they will be taken literally – for instance, do not say 'It's raining cats and dogs'.
- Teach skills that will help learners make choices – this should support individuals in widening out from an intense or obsessive focus on items that they find of interest.

Learners with dyslexia

The website of the British Dyslexia Association (**bdadyslexia.org.uk**) is a great starting point for educators needing to learn more about dyslexia and how it impacts on learners in the classroom. The term dyslexia describes a specific learning difficulty, which causes difficulty with reading and writing. Learners with dyslexia will often confuse the order of letters in words, or write letters the wrong way around. Learners who have dyslexia may also have difficulty with planning and organisation.

Many of the strategies that work well for learners with dyslexia will support all your learners, and particularly those learners with other kinds of SEND. To differentiate for learners who have dyslexia, try to:

- seat them near the front of the classroom, in a place where they have a clear view of the board
- aim for a quiet working environment, in order to support their concentration, especially when writing
- give one instruction at a time and, if appropriate, offer a note-taker
- allow plenty of time for the learners to process instructions
- consider other approaches to written expression, for instance giving a learner someone to scribe for them, using a recording device or speech-to-text software
- provide a copy of your notes and possibly also of your lesson plan, for older learners
- encourage them to record information in lots of different ways – diagrams, bullet points and images, as well as writing
- use mnemonics to help with tasks that involve a heavy load on memory
- use cues to support understanding, such as highlighting or using an asterix for important words
- encourage peer sharing, for instance of notes

- use a multisensory approach to help understanding, particularly for tasks that involve a lot of written content
- do not ask the learners to multitask.

Learners with ADHD

ADHD is a neurodevelopmental disorder that affects the parts of the brain controlling attention, impulses and concentration. Learners with ADHD will show disruptive behaviours that you would not normally expect in a learner of a similar age and development. Learners with ADHD will often have difficulties in other areas of learning as well. Learners with a diagnosis of ADHD may be given medication such as methylphenidate (often called *Ritalin*) to manage their symptoms. Best practice for learners with ADHD will include:

- offering multisensory activities to support focus and engagement
- keeping them hands-on with learning, and offering movement breaks whenever possible
- supporting them in developing their organisational skills, using clear routines and boundaries
- aiming for a calm and quiet working atmosphere in your classroom
- pausing and waiting for eye contact when questioning them
- using an individual's name to gain their attention
- offering some opportunities for time to daydream and be 'off task' during the school day
- teaching them strategies to monitor and manage their own behaviour, and also self-calming activities.

Learners with working memory problems

Learners with particular types of SEND will have problems with working memory – they will find it very difficult to retain information and manipulate it, even for short periods of time. This makes being in school very challenging for them, because a lot of what we ask learners to do in the classroom will put a significant strain on their working memory. For instance, a series of verbal instructions can be hard for learners to retain, and they might find it especially difficult to complete mental maths tasks. You can usually tell the learners who are having problems with working memory, because:

- They find it hard to recall something accurately, even just after they have been told it, for instance forgetting some of the words in a sentence you have just said to them.

- They struggle to follow instructions, or are only able to remember one part of what you have asked them to do.
- They ask you to repeat instructions, even though you have given them clearly.
- They repeat or skip letters or words during a sentence, or fail to complete parts of a task.
- They give up on an activity without completing it, but not because of an apparent lack of motivation or interest.

In order to differentiate for and support learners who have issues with their working memory, the following strategies are known to be helpful. Many of these strategies will also act as 'good practice' for all of your learners, in the context of your general classroom teaching.

- Keep an eye on particular learners when you have asked the class to do something that will put a load on their working memory – ask them to articulate what they have to do next to check to see if they are managing.
- Remind them that they can ask you to repeat the information as and when required – no matter how natural it might be to do so, try not to get irritated that they seem to keep asking you the same things over and over again.
- Break down tasks into smaller components and give them a visual cue for each step of what they have been asked to do – this could go on the whiteboard to support all your learners.
- Consider how much load the activities you set will have on working memory, before you set them. For instance, a series of unrelated pieces of content will be much harder to retain than a series of linked items.
- Keep your instructions clear, simple and to the point, using active rather than passive statements about what you want your learners to do.
- Allow them to make notes or scribble diagrams as you give instructions, to support them in remembering what they have to do and in what sequence.
- When giving instructions, make sure that you repeat yourself, and encourage the learners to repeat what you have said back to you, to ensure that you were clear in what you said in the first place.

Learners with EAL

Almost one in five (1.25 million) children in England are classed as having EAL. When you work with learners who have EAL, any written or spoken communication has the potential to create a barrier to learning. It is vital, therefore, that we consider how best to differentiate for these learners so that they can access the curriculum at the same time as learning a whole new language. However, it is important to remember that having EAL is not the same thing as having a learning difficulty or SEND. There is no reason why a learner with EAL could not be the highest-attaining learner in your classroom; it's just that it might be trickier for you to find this out. Equally, it is important to remember that learners who have EAL may also have learning difficulties, and again this can be harder to ascertain due to the language barrier. Lack of language is not the same thing as lack of attainment, although the two can easily be confused.

Di Leedham is an independent English, literacy and EAL teacher (@DiLeed on Twitter). She has identified three key principles that teachers need to remember when they are working with learners who have EAL: access, challenge and language development. We need to make sure that learners can access the learning and the curriculum; that we give them sufficient cognitive challenge, regardless of any language barriers; and we must also support them in developing their English, remembering that they will be learning everyday, specialist and technical language and using it for academic purposes. Di Leedham has kindly given permission for me to include the following list of her recommendations for advice and support:

- **Join NALDIC – the national subject association for English as an additional language:** You could take up individual membership or ask the leadership team at your school to join. Visit the NALDIC website (**naldic.org.uk**) for access to extensive resources about working with EAL learners.
- **Visit the British Council's EAL Nexus website:** To find lots of great ideas for working with learners who have EAL (**eal.britishcouncil.org**). This website includes ideas that you can share with parents as well as useful ideas for all teachers.
- **Look at Hampshire's Young Interpreter Scheme (YIS):** This scheme offers a great way to support young people in helping their peers and supporting their language development until they are fully fluent in all modes of academic English needed. Visit **www3.hants.gov.uk/hyis** or see @YIScheme on Twitter to find out more.

In terms of your day-to-day classroom practice, there are a number of things that you can do to differentiate for learners who have EAL. The strategies you use will vary according to the subject you are teaching and the phase you are working in. Remember that, at the same time as they are learning a second language, and learning the curriculum, your EAL learners will also be learning and developing in their first language as well.

Starting points

As with all aspects of differentiation, the key starting point is to find out more about your learners. If you are teaching in England, your school should provide you with statutory DfE codes that identify the individual learner's level of proficiency in English (these are based on pre-existing codes from Wales). Bear in mind that the accuracy of these codes will depend on the expertise of the person who has been asked to assign them. In some schools there are specialist language teachers and dedicated language units, but this is by no means a universal picture. It is also important to note that these descriptors are a 'best fit' and they are not moderated, so their application will inevitably vary from school to school. You should also remember that a learner's proficiency could vary in reading, writing, speaking and listening. The EAL codes are:

- **A:** new to English
- **B:** early acquisition
- **C:** developing competence
- **D:** competent
- **E:** fluent.

Find out about the language that the learner speaks at home, either from your school or from the learner or their parents/carers. It can be very helpful to find out whether the learner was born in the UK or not, and to learn a bit more about their family circumstances. This might give you some insights into:

- the kind of education system the learner has been in thus far
- the type of cultural background the learner comes from
- whether the learner might have had traumatic experiences prior to arriving in the UK
- whether they may need social and emotional support as a result
- whether the learner was identified as having any special educational needs during their time in the education system elsewhere.

When a learner who has EAL first arrives in your class or in your setting, or when you first come to teach them, there are a number of practical steps you can take:

- **Ask how to pronounce their name, and practise saying it a number of times:** If you forget, or if you struggle with the correct pronunciation, ask again until you get the hang of it. No matter how tricky you find the pronunciation, it's far, far better to ask for clarification than to say someone's name incorrectly.
- **Offer a list of 'survival words' – words that we need immediately on arriving somewhere new:** Depending on the age of the learner, you could make a written list with visuals, a translated list with words, or you could record these key words for the learner to learn. Survival words would include 'yes', 'no', 'thank you', 'food', 'drink', 'toilet', 'help'.

- **Encourage the learner to use gestures to communicate, and use lots of gestures in return:** Think about how we behave when we are in a country where we don't speak the language – we tend to point at things, gesticulate, and use much more exaggerated facial expressions than we normally would.
- **Add symbols and visuals all around your classroom, to support understanding:** Label drawers with an image of what is inside, as well as writing the name of the contents on the label.
- **Where possible, provide a translator, especially early on when they don't have much English at all:** This could be a member of the learner's own family (e.g. a parent), another learner in your class with the same language but with a greater grasp of English, or a technological tool such as an app.
- **Bear in mind that they will need to get around at break times, as well as getting to classes:** Ask for a volunteer to buddy up with them when they arrive in your setting; if possible, find someone who shares the same home language.

Thinking about language

Di Leedham emphasises that, when you teach learners who have EAL, you need to talk to them and teach them about language, as well as about the lesson subject. In order to learn a new language, we need to understand its internal structures. It's important to remember that some languages operate very differently from English – the writing system may be entirely different, the grammatical constructions may be the complete inverse of those in English, or the pronunciation may vary significantly. We are born with the potential to speak any language – it is when we learn our first language as babies that we develop the muscles in our faces needed to pronounce it. Your EAL learners will need to repeat this process for English as a second or additional language. Make sure that you:

- **Consider the types of language that learners with EAL will need to learn in your lessons – everyday language, specialist words and technical terminology:** Unlike when we learn a foreign language in school, where the emphasis is more on getting by in a foreign country, your learners will be required to communicate in their new language in an academic manner.
- **When providing key word lists, make sure that you separate these out into logical groups and types of words:** Depending on the context, you might sort them by word type (noun, verb, adjective, etc.) or separate them because they are linked in some other way, for instance words that have similar meanings.
- **When providing a list of words, think about how you lay them out:** You might create a semantic web to show how the words link to each other.

You could put the simplest or most important word for the lesson at the top of the page, then show how it links to more complicated words by the use of arrows or other symbols. Add visuals to word lists whenever possible.

- **Consider colour-coding language to support understanding:** For instance, you might highlight all the verbs in a piece of writing in one colour, and all the nouns in another.
- **Consider pronunciation:** Bear in mind that, depending on the learner's mother tongue, they might find some words in English extremely difficult to pronounce.

Thinking about talk

In the classroom, you as the teacher provide a very useful model of talk for learners with EAL (and, indeed, for all your learners). The way that you communicate with your class will have a direct impact on how well the learners understand what you are saying, whatever their first language is. When you are whole-class teaching, or leading whole-class discussions, there are some simple strategies that will ensure that your learners will understand as much as possible of what you are saying:

- Speak clearly and not too quickly, and enunciate your words carefully.
- Use plenty of repetition, particularly when explaining important ideas or when giving instructions.
- As you repeat an idea or an instruction, adapt the vocabulary slightly to build the level of challenge for your learners.
- Face the class whenever you can, so that your learners can see your face.
- Incorporate facial expressions and gestures into your talk to support meaning.
- Where possible, avoid idiomatic expressions (expressions that are particular to a language and which may not translate directly or at all). Aim to use words in their most literal way.

Self talk and parallel talk are both very useful methods for supporting language learning (when learning both a first and a second language). The term 'self talk' describes the process whereby the teacher narrates what they are doing as they do it, e.g. 'First, let's open your book to page ten and then we can try to read the passage together.' The term 'parallel talk' describes the process whereby the teacher narrates what the learner is doing as they do it, e.g. 'I see you are playing with the red ball. You dropped the red ball.' It can feel a bit odd when you do this, particularly at first, but it really is very helpful for learners who are new to English, as they hear you modelling the way that the new language works.

Open discussions can be tricky for learners who have EAL, because they don't have the vocabulary that they might need to understand or to join in. At the same time, though, your learners need plenty of chances to hear and rehearse talk, in low-pressure situations. Working in a small group is one way to facilitate this. Bear in mind the following advice about group work for learners with EAL:

- **Give the learners scaffolds to use when you ask them to communicate with a group, and plan for how each learner is going to be able to contribute:** A substitution table is a very useful device to achieve this. This is a table that gives model sentences, with a range of choices for learners to select from, using a set pattern. For instance: 'The circle/square/triangle is red/blue/green.' A substitution table allows learners to practise their English in independent contexts, both spoken and written, even when they are fairly new to the language. You can find out more about substitution tables on the British Council's EAL Nexus website (see eal.britishcouncil.org/teachers/great-ideas-substitution-tables).
- **Some learners will prefer to stay silent until they are fairly comfortable in a new language, even in a small-group situation:** This is not the learner trying to be awkward; it is simply a different response to the experience of language-learning. Try not to react in a negative way to a learner who prefers not to talk. Consider how you would feel about speaking in a language that is not your own, in a classroom situation, in order to help you empathise with them.
- **If you have several learners who speak the same home language, consider whether you might allow them to communicate in their first language during some kinds of group tasks:** This can be useful in an activity in which you want the learners to be able to discuss and capture their thoughts, because it allows them to converse much more freely. After their initial discussion, the learners could move to work with a talk partner in English, to reformulate their ideas from their home language.

Best practice in the EAL classroom

There are plenty of ways that you can adapt for and support the learning of learners with EAL in your classroom, on a day-to-day basis. Many of the techniques given below will also be useful for learners who have SEND or generally for learners who need differentiated support to access the learning. The main aim is to overcome the language barrier that gets in the way of learners having access to meaning.

- **Aim to pre-teach content for your lessons wherever possible:** This is so that the learners have already 'met' some of the vocabulary before they get to class. You might offer online resources, or a list of key words that are likely to help the learners in class.

- **Diagrams, images and symbols are very powerful for sharing meaning without language:** Aim to provide images that support the learning that is going on in your lesson at a conceptual level, e.g. not just an image of a frog, but an image of the life cycle of the frog.
- **Provide core words for each lesson, especially technical ones, which typically take much longer for someone to learn in a new language:** You could make a visual dictionary of the key words in the subject and let the learners have this ahead of time.
- **Give learners lots and lots of chances to rehearse language:** This should be with both you and their peers, in low-pressure situations.
- **When you are working with text, offer texts with the most important words underlined or highlighted:** You could also offer simplified or translated versions of texts, or a translated version for a learner with little or no English. It can be very useful to offer these to the learner to read before the lesson takes place. However, take care with Google Translate, and do not assume that it will render you a correct translation.
- **When you are whole-class teaching, it is important to maintain the flow of your lesson:** However, at the same time you might need to go over vocabulary with individuals later on. Ask the learners to capture examples of words or phrases that they don't fully understand on a sheet of paper or a mini whiteboard. You can then explain these to the learners when everyone else is on task, later on in the lesson.
- **Remember that language learning is linked to the motivation of the individual:** Encourage your learners to take responsibility for their own language learning. For instance, you could give them a notebook in which they can note down words they would like to know about, and encourage them to carry a small dictionary with them at all times.
- **Be conscious that EAL learners might acquire specialist words before everyday ones:** This is because they are learning the language mainly in an academic classroom context. Don't be surprised if you find yourself needing to explain what seem to be fairly simple words, especially ones that don't appear in the same way in the learner's original culture. For instance, a learner might never have come across the term 'afternoon tea'.
- **Bear in mind the cultural differences that exist at a more fundamental and conceptual level:** For instance, the way that different countries view the symbolism of colour. Did you know that in China, white and not black is the colour of mourning? Remember that your learners might be too polite to point this out to you and so you will not necessarily realise that they don't understand the concept you are trying to explain.

- **Don't forget to support your learners who are three or four years into the process of learning English:** While you're busy differentiating for your new language learners, do not forget that your more advanced EAL learners might need additional support. A smart intervention, timed for when the learner is really starting to get to grips with English, can boost academic performance.

Be conscious that it is very tiring to try to communicate in another language all day long, especially when you are completely new to it. You have to listen very carefully and effectively and you must translate what you hear into your own language, then back again into English, before you can respond to it. You may find that those learners who have EAL seem to get very tired in the last lesson of the day. Take account of this in the way that you plan for learning.

Home–school communication

Parents and carers are a fantastic source of information about how well the approaches you are using are working for their children (or not). When educators are able to work in conjunction with families, this can be a great support for better learning in the classroom. However, it is often the case that we under-utilise them as a resource. This can be partly to do with time and workload, but perhaps it is also sometimes to do with an uncertainty about how to go about approaching them. There are lots of strategies that you can use to enhance home–school communication, in order to better differentiate for your learners. Here are a few thoughts:

- **Ask them!:** Often it is simply a case of asking parents/carers to tell you more about what is going on in their child's life that might be causing any issues that you face in your classroom.
- **Get information from them, for instance sending out questionnaires to find out their views:** A simple and straightforward technique is to ask parents to write a short note at the end of their child's homework, saying how they approached it, which bits they found difficult, whether the parent feels they made sufficient effort, and so on.
- **Let them know what they can do to support you:** Think of your parents and carers as learners, just like your learners themselves. Send home information about early reading, about supporting homework, about revising for exams, etc.
- **Don't let yourself be put off by the thought that the parents/carers of your learners might not be interested in contributing to their child's education:** Even if only a handful of parents/carers give you feedback, this is still better than none at all.

- **Remember that they are probably more nervous of you than you are of them:** Even as someone who has worked 'in the trade' for years, I still find it a little bit nerve-racking to speak to my own children's teachers.

Parents and carers of learners with SEND can be an absolute gold mine of information about their child and their child's condition. Unfortunately, it can sometimes be the case that schools consider parents to be 'awkward' or 'difficult' when they push for additional support for their child. A family who has an EHCP for their child will have spent significant time understanding what their child's problems are, and how they can best be supported in their learning. We would do well to listen to them as fully as we possibly can.

The better that we understand who our different learners are, and what particular needs and skills they bring with them when they come into our classrooms, the better placed we will be to differentiate effectively for them.

Chapter 4
The teacher and the teaching

Although differentiation is in part about planning ahead and thinking through the options for teaching and learning before a lesson takes place, it is also very much about reacting to what happens in a classroom situation. If an approach isn't working, in the sense that the learners are not learning what you had intended, then you need to develop the ability to adapt what you had planned in the moment. In this section I look at the many subtle adaptations that teachers can make during the course of a lesson or a session of learning, to ensure that they meet the needs of all their learners. These adaptations include both the way that the teacher presents the learning to the learners, and also the way that the teacher behaves – for instance how they use their voice and body, how they handle behaviour and how they create routines for learning.

It is useful to remember that you will *already be differentiating* the aspects of your practice described in this chapter, even if you are not aware that this is what you are doing. So many of the processes involved become subconscious that it is easy to underestimate the complexity of the approaches you already have in place. See how often you can 'catch yourself' responding to your learners and adapting in the moment – that flexibility is at the heart of all good teaching, because education is essentially about a relationship with the people in front of you, rather than some mythical group of learners that you might have thought you would get to teach some day.

These days, it is often the case that there will be more than one adult in the classroom. Alongside the teacher there might also be a teaching assistant, a learning support assistant, or perhaps a learning mentor. Most of the time, the most highly skilled person in the classroom will be the teacher, and it's important to remember this when you are thinking about who should work with the learners with the highest level of need. It is also well worth reflecting on your own thought processes around the subject of differentiation, because these will influence the way that you work with your learners in your classroom.

Teacher attitudes

The way that you feel about your learners will influence the way that you teach them. You might hope that it would not, and you can certainly try your hardest not to let it become a negative in your teaching, but it is best not to ignore it as a possibility. This influence can be subtle, and you might not always be conscious that it is even happening, but it will inevitably have an impact on what you do in your classroom. Differentiation has the potential to cause additional workload for teachers, particularly if the pressure from your school is to do lots of differentiation by task or by resources. The time pressures that this causes might colour your feelings about differentiation more generally.

Take a moment to consider your own attitudes about:

- what 'differences' there are or might be between your learners
- what each of your learners is capable of achieving
- who has or should have 'ownership' of your classroom and the learning that happens within it
- who decides on the direction of travel of the learning – is it always the teacher to the learners, or can learning go in both directions?

On the plus side, differentiation is about a belief in what learners can achieve. It is about having respect for the learners – the diversity of who and what they are at the moment, as well as who and what they will become in the future. Differentiation is an invitation for learners to participate in lessons and a statement that their needs, wishes and interests are valued. It is an investment in your classroom and in making your lessons feel like a good place to be. On the downside, differentiation is likely to add to your workload – it would probably be a lot easier to teach a single set of ideas to your learners using the same approach for everyone. There is also the potential for differentiation to limit your expectations of what the learners might achieve, because it can be hard to pitch your approach at exactly the right level, so that everyone is challenged, while everyone is also supported.

The importance of self-reflection

There is a handy quote that is often used in relation to differentiation, which goes something like this: 'If you've told a child a thousand times and he still does not understand, then it is not the child who is the slow learner.' (Walter Barbe) One of the key factors for effective differentiation is a willingness to reflect on what you yourself do, and to go through a process of self-evaluation. When you have taught something, but the learners have not learnt it, you might blame them for not making enough effort or not listening, but you can also look at your own practice in detail and consider what you might be able to change and adapt. This is categorically not blaming the teacher for a lack of effort on the part of the learners; rather, it is saying that your own approach is the thing over which you have most control.

You will need persistence to keep on trying to match the learning to the learners, even where they seem to reject your efforts, or they do not appreciate how much trouble you are taking. With all the other pressures of the job, and of your workload, it might be tempting to give up trying. At the same time, though, a willingness to look at your own practice critically opens up the space for you to learn and develop as a teacher. What did you do, and how did it impact on the learning? What did you do well, and what could you improve the next time around?

Modelling

When you need your learners to work on a new skill or activity, you will want to model it for them first. By providing them with a clear model of how the new skill works, how the concept can be understood, or how the activity should be completed, you pass on as much information as possible before you hand it over to them to practise it. As you model a task for your learners, you can use all sorts of teaching strategies that will support the varying needs of the learners in your class:

- **Think out loud as you model the process you are going through:** This kind of metacognition (talking about our own thinking) is very powerful in supporting learning. It will be particularly helpful for those learners who struggle to conceptualise new ideas.
- **Get examples from the class to ensure that they understand what you are saying:** Think carefully about which learners you choose to give the examples, as this will give you an insight into their thinking and can boost motivation for the learners. Who needs a boost to their confidence? Who looks a bit puzzled but has a hand up and is keen to contribute anyway?
- **Repeat the activity you are modelling several times over if necessary:** Get lots of different examples from your learners, and preferably get them involved in the writing or modelling itself. Don't assume that all learners will see something once and understand it immediately. This is especially important for learners with specific types of SEND.
- **If you have learners who you know are already capable at this skill, or learners who will have understood first time around, you might send them away to start on the activity:** They could sit and work on an activity supervised by a TA, or on their own, while you continue to model examples with the rest of the class or with a smaller group.

- **Film yourself modelling the process:** A useful alternative to repeated modelling is to film yourself modelling the process (for instance a science experiment) and then to replay the film in class on your interactive whiteboard, for the learners to watch as often as they need.
- **Use visuals such as symbols, as well as words, to support understanding for those learners who might struggle with language:** For example, if you are brainstorming a list of thoughts for and against an idea, you might put a tick at the top of one column to show 'positives' and a cross at the top of the other to show 'negatives'.

Giving instructions

It is surprisingly hard to give clear instructions that all your learners will understand. When there are misunderstandings, this can lead to all sorts of confusion and time wasted as learners demand to know, 'What did you say we should do again?' It is worth thinking through a set of instructions before you give them, and considering how you will ensure that every learner in the class understands what it is that you want them to do. There is no harm in framing instructions very clearly indeed – even those who would have understood a slightly more vague explanation will appreciate the clarity. Consider how many instructions you might want to give at one time, and to which learners.

One of the key points at which the learners will often get sidetracked from what they are meant to be learning is when they are moving from the teacher-led part of the lesson to the part of the lesson in which they are expected to work independently. The key is to give the instructions in such a way that your learners are completely clear about what they are meant to be doing. This helps you avoid lots of learners asking for clarification in the immediate period after you have set them off to work. Some learners will find it easier than others to retain the instructions you give, so you could well need to differentiate your approaches. For those learners who struggle to retain detail when you are giving instructions, it can be useful to:

- break the instruction down into small parts
- use short sentences to explain what you want them to do
- give the instructions in sequence, thinking carefully about the order in which to present them
- take your learners through the steps needed to get the resources ready for the task (books out, pen out, write the title and date, or get into groups, etc.) before you explain what the task is

- use lots of repetition – ask the learners to repeat back what you have asked before you set them off to do it, especially where you are giving a longer list of instructions
- back up your instructions with lots of visual cues and clues, e.g. a hand gesture of the learners joining together, to indicate that you want them to work in a group, or three fingers in the air when you want them to answer three questions
- offer a set of visual cues on your whiteboard, written in chronological order – this could take the form of a diagram rather than written information.

Sometimes you will need to give quite a complex set of instructions, and for some of your learners it will be very hard to retain the full set in one go. A very useful technique to use when giving long sets of instructions is to break them down into smaller parts, getting the learners to do each part before you move onto the next. When you do this, you are basically scaffolding the instruction-giving process for them. For instance, you might say:

- First, please could everybody open their exercise books and get out a pen.
- Now, please write the title and date, just like I am writing it on the whiteboard.
- Next, can everybody open their text book at page ten.
- Now, complete questions one to five.

I find that it often works best not to say what the task itself is until the learners have understood everything they need to know about how they are going to approach it. The minute you let your learners know what the task is going to be, their focus turns to that and you lose their attention for any explanations about how to use resources, set out the work, and so on. Your learners may even start to try to complete work before you have actually finished explaining it. To avoid this, it is useful to use the following pattern:

- First, give any instructions about how to handle resources.
- Next, explain what kind of format they will work in – individually, in pairs, in small groups, and so on.
- Now, set any targets or give any information about timing, e.g. at least ten ideas; you only have three minutes, and so on.
- Finally, tell them what the task actually is.

It can be tricky to give instructions about an activity to a class if not all your learners are going to be doing the same thing. In order to overcome this issue, you could give written instructions to different groups, or you could explain the task to a small group who are working on something different, once everyone else is busy on task.

Developing vocabulary

One of the key differences between learners is often in the breadth and complexity of the vocabulary that they can understand and use. You may have noticed how your higher attainers tend to have a wider vocabulary of more challenging words, while your strugglers often have a more limited set of words available to use. In addition, the grammatical constructions within the learners' language will vary in complexity as well. Some learners will tend to communicate using very informal grammar, often having picked this up at home, or from their peer group. The kind of vocabulary learners use, and the way that they structure their speech, can impact on their writing and their understanding of texts, and also on the complexity of their thinking as well. It is often said that you cannot write what you cannot say, and this is very true – oral expression feeds into writing. The effect of vocabulary on the thinking processes that a learner can undertake has been noted from a very young age.

Helping learners to develop their vocabulary is not a simple process. You cannot just get your learners to memorise lots of new words and their meanings, and then expect them to be able to use these new words properly in context from that point onwards. New words are best assimilated within context, so that they fit into a broader network of understanding (sometimes referred to as a 'schema'). It is important for language to be modelled by the people around a learner for that learner to pick up on those patterns of speech long term. When it comes to more complex words, learners may need to hear them being used several times, and in a variety of contexts, to fully understand them and to start to be able to use them spontaneously. Although it is perfectly possible to give learners lists of vocabulary to learn, for long-term retention and usage it is best, where possible, for learners to experience and use new words in context.

In the first few years of their lives, children pick up the foundations of an entire language, through hearing it spoken and modelled in different situations. The wider the range of experiences the child has, the more different words they hear being spoken in context, and the more often they hear conversation and are conversed with, the more language they tend to pick up. This early period is not just about them acquiring vocabulary – they also develop an innate understanding of the grammar of their native tongue during these years as well. At first, their progress appears quite slow – babies babble, but it takes a year or more for small children to produce coherent speech. However, once they get going, their rate of word acquisition is typically exponential, especially if they are brought up in a language-rich environment. Despite never having any instruction in how to speak, and having to figure out what words mean basically through a process of deduction, children pick up their language from being immersed in it.

It is worth remembering how early language acquisition happens when you are thinking about how to differentiate for language development later on. One of the most important factors is that your learners hear you (and other adults) modelling new vocabulary in a variety of (preferably true to life) situations. Get your learners to use vocabulary, and acquire new words, in different contexts and for a variety of purposes. You could:

- **Create specific scenarios where they get to use new vocabulary in context:** For instance, in role plays, drama-based approaches and scenario-based learning. Think about how your learners will actually acquire new language in these situations – depending on their age and situation, the teacher may need to bring the new words into the situation, for instance via talk or questioning, or the learners may develop it through hearing their peers use it.
- **Take your learners out of the school environment and to places where they can be immersed in different real-life contexts:** When you are thinking about the most appropriate trips to go on, consider what kind of experiences learners with the highest levels of need might have missed. Before your journey you could introduce some of the key words to describe what you will see and experience, then use these words on the day. After the trip, you could brainstorm the new words that the learners have acquired and get them to use them within the context of a piece of writing.
- **Use texts that introduce new vocabulary in a specific context:** For instance, looking through a set of leaflets in preparation for a visit to a museum or studying travel guides before going on a school trip.
- **Explore the vocabulary that is encountered within stories:** Typically, this will be much more challenging than that which is encountered in day-to-day speech.
- **Introduce your learners to the concept of etymology:** Get them to explore the origins of the words that they use.
- **Challenge your learners by introducing a 'word of the day/week':** Ask them to use it wherever they can in their writing.
- **Encourage them to ask whenever they encounter a word that they don't understand:** Don't assume that they will fully understand every word when they are reading. Instead of disrupting the flow of their reading while it is happening, you could ask them simply to put a dot by the words for which they would like clarification.
- **Use concrete examples and objects in class, to help any new vocabulary stick:** Find ways to explain abstract words in a concrete way, for instance giving examples of ironic situations to clarify the meaning of the word 'irony'.

- **Create striking and interesting scenarios to build vocabulary and to encourage your learners to use a wider range of words:** For instance, I once met a teacher who had held a funeral with her class for the word 'nice'. The class literally went outside and buried the word 'nice' in the ground, and from that point on they were challenged to use more interesting alternatives.

Do not underestimate how capable your learners are of acquiring and using new words. If you consider for a moment how young children can learn the tricky names of a wide range of dinosaurs, you will see that, given the right motivation, they are capable of a great deal.

Variety of vocabulary

The other strategy that you can use in lessons is to vary the complexity of the vocabulary that you use with your learners, in a scale moving from the simple to the complex. This is not to say that you should only ever use simple words with those learners who have a limited vocabulary and save the complex words for learners who have a more advanced vocabulary. Instead, what you can do is to use enough repetition to say the same thing in different ways, to ensure all your learners understand what you mean and can pick up on new ways of describing things. You can also adapt the conceptual complexity of your vocabulary according to the learners you are talking with at any given moment.

Varying your vocabulary is a subtle form of differentiation, and it is one that an observer might not even notice that you are using. It involves explaining things in such a way that everyone understands them. You might need to point out that you are deliberately using this as a strategy, or include information about how you have considered different levels of language for conceptualisation in your lesson planning. What might varying levels of vocabulary look like?

- When talking about money, you might also use the words 'currency' and 'denomination'.
- When working on maths, you might use the words 'minus', 'take away' and 'subtract'.
- When talking about how a writer conveys meaning, you might use a range of words, including 'implies', 'suggests', 'infers' and 'connotes'.

Routines for learning

One of the key ways that you can support your learners' learning is by having clear routines in your classroom – not only for behaviour, but also for learning. We often think of routines as being used for classroom management, for instance getting the learners to come into and out of the room sensibly, but routines can also usefully be linked to learning as well. Having routines for learning is a great way to support differentiation, because it increases both the level of challenge and the amount of support at the same time. The key point about your routines is that they should be designed to help the learners become more independent in their learning – to answer questions for themselves whenever they can. After all, we don't want the teacher to take all the responsibility for doing this; we want the learners to sort as much out for themselves as they possibly can. In the same way that we need to take scaffolds away as quickly as we can, to ensure that learners don't become overdependent on them, so we need in the end to encourage our learners to move beyond the need for teacher-led routines.

When you think about which learners in your class or classes need routines, and why they might need them, you will quickly see that this kind of thinking is all about differentiation. Some of your learners will need much more support than others, and this support might take the form of clarity around classroom routines, as well as clarity around the learning.

What should I do if I need help?

When learners constantly come to you asking for help, this can give you a useful insight into other issues that might be going on with their learning. It could be that a learner is coming to you for help all the time in order to gain adult attention, in which case you might want to consider how you could give that learner attention for more positive behaviours. It may be that a learner lacks confidence around their learning, and that you may need to plan for ways to boost their self-esteem. Perhaps the learner needs more support with the activity you have set or you need to differentiate the task for them more fully. You will need to use your judgement to decide whether any of these are the case.

Because we all love our learners to ask questions, it is very tempting to answer every question we are ever asked. However, this tends to encourage our learners into the habit of asking far too many questions, rather than thinking for themselves. As a teacher you need to develop selective hearing – if a learner asks you a question that you know they could easily answer for themselves, have a routine stock response. You could try saying something like 'Think again', or you could simply ignore the question altogether. The learners will soon get the message that it is pointless trying to ask you pointless questions to which they should already know the answer. Here are some other ideas to try:

- **Teach your learners to use 'three before me':** Explain to them that they must try at least three strategies to find help before they ask an adult. These strategies could include: asking a classmate, thinking again, looking it up in a book, finding the correct spelling in a dictionary, looking back over the work they've done in the past to see if they had this problem before.

- **Instigate a tickets-for-questions system:** This is another great way to limit the number of pointless questions you get asked and to encourage your learners to carefully consider whether or not their question needs asking. Give each learner a number of raffle tickets (this could perhaps range from one to three tickets). Now explain to them that, every time they ask you a question, they have to cash in one of their tickets. This helps to make them think ahead about how important their question is.
- **Help your learners learn to rephrase the questions they ask you as statements:** This will encourage them to think through what the problem holding them up actually is, rather than coming to you and expecting an instant solution. So, instead of asking you 'Is this okay?', they must make a specific statement instead, e.g. 'I'm not sure whether I've given enough detail here.'
- **Try answering your learners' questions with a question, rather than an answer:** You could use questions like 'What do you think?' or 'Can you think of a way to solve that?'
- **Help your learners avoid attention-seeking through helplessness by identifying and praising examples of learners who are doing something more positive:** If an individual comes to you to ask for help, before you give it to them, look around the room and say, 'I see James is using three before me, and Jazmeena is clarifying the activity for her partner, thank you both.' You might find that this is enough to encourage the individual to go and figure out what to do on their own.
- **At the same time, make sure that you don't put some learners off from asking questions completely:** This is especially important for those learners who might be really struggling to understand what is being asked of them, but who lack the confidence to come to ask you for clarification. If you know there are some individuals in a group that tend not to ask when they need help, you could go to each individual and ask if they are clear, immediately after setting a task.

I've finished – what do I do now?

This is a question that your learners should never need to ask, especially if you have planned ahead for early finishers. If you always plan to top and tail your lessons (see Chapter 1, page 15), there will always be an extension task available for those who have worked quickly and a support for those who need it. If you have a clear set of routines around the idea of what a 'finished' piece of work looks like, and what to do next after completing it, you can meet this question with an inscrutable silence, with a knowing smile, or by pointing to a sign on your wall. Here are some other ideas to try:

- **Have a set of non-negotiables for any claim from an individual that a piece of work is 'finished':** These can be linked into your expectations of things like presentation – for instance, you could insist that learners must proofread their work and ensure that it has a date and a title, underlined, before they are allowed to tell you that it's finished. You could put a list up on your wall of all the things you want your learners to check for themselves, so that you can refer to it non-verbally whenever an individual comes to you claiming a piece of work they have done is complete.
- **Create an extension box, in which you store a set of tasks that a learner can access without any teacher input:** You could focus on fun, generic activities such as quizzes or puzzles, or you might choose to put in subject-related extension tasks. Your extension activities should be ones that can be done independently of the teacher, or otherwise you will be creating an additional workload for yourself in explaining them.
- **Encourage your learners to think about reviewing and critiquing their own work when they feel it is complete:** You could give them a format within which to do this – for instance, asking them to check their work against a mark scheme, or to swap books with a friend to give them some feedback.
- **Give clear instructions about where the learners should put their finished work, to avoid them having to come to you to ask this question:** This might be in a tray, in a pile on your desk, in a drawer for books from that subject area, and so on. A handy tip for speeding up your marking is to ask your learners to leave their books open at the page they have just been writing on.

Introducing the lesson

It is really important for your learners to have a sense of where a lesson is going, ahead of time – both what they will be doing, and also what they will be learning. This is especially important if you have learners in your class who have certain types of SEND, such as being on the autistic spectrum, because it gives them a sense of structure to the lesson time. The way that you introduce the lesson and explain what they are going to be learning will help them map out in their heads the progress of the session and the concepts or skills they will be learning. It can also reassure the learners about how they might feel during different parts of the lesson.

If a learner in your class struggles to sit still and listen for long periods, being told that there will only be a short introduction should help them focus during that time. You could even make the amount of time visual for them, by using a sand timer or other timing device. Aim to become conscious of how different learners might respond to the introductory part of your lesson, as this is all part of good differentiation. If you can incorporate strategies to support them, this is likely to lead to a much more effective lesson. There are lots of different ways that you can help your learners see what the shape of the lesson will be. You might:

- use a picture sequence to show each step of a lesson on your whiteboard
- talk the class through the activities that will go on during your time together
- list the activities and the time for each one in a column at the side of your whiteboard
- share an object or item that you plan to use to explain the concepts
- create a personal 'timetable' of the lesson for individuals who might need it – if you laminate this they could tick off each part of the lesson as it happens.

When you are introducing the lesson, think about the needs of your different learners in terms of their concentration and understanding. It is probably best not to assume that everyone will understand the objective and the content fully from an oral explanation, especially if you have any learners in your class who struggle to concentrate on teacher talk or who have problems with their working memory. A visual back-up to support your explanation is always going to be useful and it certainly can't do any harm. When you ask for volunteers to help you demonstrate or model an activity, consider choosing those learners who like to be active in their learning, to give them a chance to move during the introductory phase of the lesson.

Visuals and organising information

There are many different ways that you can organise information in order to make it more accessible for your learners. A lot of these approaches will be things you would do instinctively for a whole class, but you can use them specifically to support understanding for individuals as well. In terms of the ways that people take in meaning, a page of plain text, written in paragraph blocks, is probably the hardest format to read for understanding. Adding images, symbols and diagrams can support understanding for learners with different kinds of needs. To help learners who struggle to read large blocks of text, you might use:

- diagrams with labels – for instance, to explain the water cycle in geography
- timelines with images – for instance, to show the sequence of events in history
- mind maps to show how ideas or themes link to each other – for example, in a play in literature
- highlighted sections or boxed wording, to draw attention to particular parts of the writing – for example, in a report in business studies.

Graphics organiser

A 'graphics organiser' offers a way to combine words with images, in order to help learners understand and remember things better. By seeing something in two formats – both visual and lexical – this helps the learners sift through the information, figure out what it means and remember it better. Diagrams and images work best when any text is incorporated into the diagram itself, rather than presented to one side of it as a separate entity. Presenting the information in this way helps your learners form the networks of understanding that are needed to retain it. When you are creating graphics organisers, it is a good idea to:

- integrate the text into the visuals, rather than separating the two out
- organise the information into a hierarchy with the most important ideas at the top, or on the left
- use a larger font for more important ideas, to help clarify their importance, with the font gradually getting smaller for less important details
- incorporate colour to help clarify meaning, for example using the colour blue for terminology connected to water.

There are various other ways to use visuals to make information easier to understand. For instance, you can:

- create semantic maps and networks – these are diagrams and images with text incorporated
- put key words in a box, to draw your learners' attention to them
- use images to clarify and aid retention of the etymology of individual words – for instance, adding a picture of a fire to the word 'igneous' to show the origin from the Latin 'ignis'
- group ideas together under different headings, to show how specific concepts are linked to each other, and to demonstrate patterns of meaning.

Another good way for your learners to remember things is to learn how to make visual representations of them in their minds. Some learners will tend to do this naturally, but others will really struggle to visualise and will benefit a great deal from input and explanation in this area.

Supporting retention

One of the key differences between your learners is in how well they will be able to remember and reuse the skills and knowledge that you have taught them. Some learners seem to find it easy to retain and manipulate information or techniques, while others struggle to remember what you have said in class, and the learning seems to drop out of their heads the moment they leave the room. No matter how many times you teach them to use a full stop, or to remember their times tables, it just doesn't seem to stick. It is well worth teaching your learners strategies to support their own skill at remembering facts, and remembering how to do things.

As explained above, visuals can help with retention, for instance putting images into a sequence to show events during a period of history, or creating a timeline of images that show how a particular activity should be undertaken. Visual timetables can also be a great help to learners with particular kinds of SEND, such as autism (see Chapter 3, page 68–9).

Retaining skills

In part, your learners' use (or not) of skills such as correct punctuation will be to do with how much they are motivated to use them. Even if they understand where a full stop should go, it doesn't necessarily follow that they will use one in their writing. It is important to differentiate between a learner who *doesn't understand* a particular skill, and one who is *poorly motivated* to demonstrate it. You may need to differentiate between the approaches you use to focus on either motivation or understanding, for different learners. To focus your energies wisely, you could:

- **Break down the skill itself with an individual, to see where the problem lies:** Before you can use full stops, you need to understand what a sentence is, and how it works for a reader. Can the learner explain to you the correct definition of a sentence? Can they identify correct and incorrect punctuation when they see it?
- **Give those learners who can already use a specific skill more freedom to work spontaneously:** For instance, while you focus on going over the use of full stops with one group, another group might do some free writing. There is no point in a learner who understands something, and can use it perfectly, spending time practising it out of context.
- **Set targets and create motivators, to encourage learners to use their skills correctly:** For instance, if a learner can punctuate a piece of writing correctly, they get to move on to the next task, or receive some kind of reward.
- **Give your learners as much responsibility as possible for correcting their own work:** Do not accept that a piece of writing is 'finished' until an individual has proofread it and corrected as many mistakes as they can on their own.

Retaining facts

For thousands of years, human beings have found ways to remember and pass on information more easily. The key factor in retaining information is to find ways to link the pieces of information you want to retrieve, one to another. By linking something that is new to your learners to something they already know, you help them place it within a schema to help them remember it. The 'Roman room' is among various memorisation strategies that date back centuries. With more and more focus on memorising large amounts of information for exams such as SATs and GCSEs, the case for teaching memory techniques to your learners grows ever stronger. Understanding how to use these techniques will be especially important for those learners with SEND who have difficulty memorising and retaining information.

There are many different strategies that you and your learners can use to support memorisation. Encourage your learners to understand how these strategies work – once again, this helps them to think about their own thinking (also referred to as metacognition). Those learners who seem to find remembering things easy may already be using some or several of these strategies, probably subconsciously. You can encourage them to devise additional approaches of their own, taking ownership of their learning. Those learners who do not use these strategies instinctively will benefit from you teaching them explicitly.

Some of the memorisation strategies that you could teach your learners to use would include:

- **Visualisation:** Encourage learners to 'see' the answer in their mind's eye, or to imagine an image that will help them to remember the answer. For instance, if they visualise 'I ate and I ate until I was sick on the floor' this could help them to remember 8 x 8 = 64.
- **Stories:** When you incorporate information into a story, this creates links between the pieces of information that will help your learners retain them. For instance, you could devise a story together in which a character goes on a journey. Along the way they encounter each of the pieces of information that they need to remember. Encourage your learners to really place themselves visually inside the story, to make the images more memorable for themselves.
- **Mnemonics:** When you're making up mnemonics, the funnier they are the better, as they will catch your learners' attention and make them easier to remember. For instance, if you can make a mnemonic that creates the word 'FART', you can be sure that your learners will not forget it! Get your learners involved in making up their own mnemonics, to show them how they can control and manage their own learning.
- **Associations:** When we link two ideas together this helps us remember them. Another well-known memory system revolves around linking new

ideas to numbers, by linking each number to a specific word. This approach works well for lists of things that need to be remembered. For instance, for the first item in the list, assign the word 'sun' (one = sun), and they can remember the new idea more easily by imagining the sun beating down on it.

- **Etymology:** This works very well as an aide memoire. For example, you could help your learners remember the meaning of the word 'photosynthesis' by seeing 'photo' and 'synthesis' as two separate entities, then imagining the plant taking a photo and synthesising light from it.
- **Grouping into categories:** This can work well for retention, for instance creating different categories of quotes based on the themes in a literary text.
- **Making links to things your learners see regularly in their day-to-day lives outside of school:** This is a powerful technique for memory. For example, you could talk about Minecraft when you are studying the four times table. The blocks in Minecraft are in units of four – how many units would be in a tower that was six blocks tall?
- **Mind mapping:** This is a technique that never seems to go out of fashion. Creating mind maps is a great way for learners to map out, structure and visualise information in their minds. Encourage them to use colours and add visuals, as this will make their mind maps more memorable. Get them to put the main concept in the centre, in a larger font, then add a related network of ideas radiating out from it.
- **Self-assessment quiz:** Encourage your learners to check how well they have remembered something by giving themselves a quick quiz as a form of self-assessment. They can then focus on remembering the bits that they got wrong, because these are more likely to be tricky for them to retain.
- **Repeated listening:** It can be very useful for memory to listen to the thing you want to remember, over and over again. This can be particularly helpful for those learners who struggle to visualise things, or who don't deal well with large blocks of text. If you think for a moment about how we remember songs, it's obvious that we retain them because we hear them so often, and also because the melodies are 'catchy'. We will even talk about our irritation at an 'earworm' – a tune that gets stuck in our heads and which we can't seem to get rid of. Utilise this by encouraging your learners to record and listen back to things like poems and quotes that they need to remember.

Teach your learners strategies for memorising; be explicit with them about the best ways to do this, especially as they move towards GCSE age. Bear in mind that the best strategies will differ according to the learner, and that you may need to encourage different learners to use different approaches.

Using stories

Stories are great for supporting learning, because they engage your learners and they help to make learning more memorable. This is not just about reading stories to a primary class, but about using stories more generally in your teaching. As noted in the list above, a story can make it much easier for us to remember complex information. This is because it helps us to visualise ideas and link them one to another. You might have noticed how, when you read a novel, you find it relatively easy to retain a complex storyline and understand the plot as you go along. As well as being of benefit for memory, you can also use stories to help you differentiate for different learners. For instance, you might:

- **Use a story that reflects personal interests:** By using a story theme that will appeal to the learners you most need to reach, this will help make it more memorable for them. For example, if a learner is really into horses, then you could base your maths learning on a story about a horse. You could link this to maths about how tall it was, how fast it went, and so on.
- **Use stories to celebrate diversity:** Ensure that the stories you use in class reflect both the learners you teach and also the wider cultural backdrop, including learners with EAL. Make sure that learners from different backgrounds see themselves represented in the stories that you share, to celebrate the difference and diversity within your own community and within our wider society.
- **Use stories to offer role models, from which different learners can learn:** By using the stories of a wide range of people, you celebrate all kinds of lives. Make sure that you show your learners stories about people with disabilities, people from diverse backgrounds, and people who have succeeded against the odds.

Offering choice

If we want our learners to feel motivated, and to focus on what they are doing, it can really help to give them a sense of ownership around their learning. If we are totally honest with ourselves, it is often the case that the teacher makes most of the decisions in the classroom. Even though we might try to harness the power of 'student voice' in our schools, it's actually rarely the case that our learners get much of a say in their learning or in the way that their schools work. The adults tend to be the ones deciding what they will learn about, at what time of day and for how long, and typically we make these decisions ahead of time. This can lead to a sense of learnt helplessness – if learners feel that they have no choice in the matter, they may as well do what the teacher says without really thinking about it.

If you are going to give your learners choices about what learning they complete, or the format in which they complete it, you need to have a certain level of trust in them. This can be tricky, especially if you work in a difficult context where some learners have a tendency to push at the limits around behaviour. On the other hand, there is no way that a learner can earn your trust unless you give it in the first place: it seems unfair to those learners who are trustworthy never to be given any trust at all. We have to be willing to risk going through the experience of being let down, before we can hope to build a sense of responsibility in our learners. When we give our learners a say in what they learn and how they learn it, this also encourages them to think about managing their own learning.

When you are using choice to support differentiation, there is no need to give your learners unlimited choice, as this can lead to confusion and difficulty with making a decision. If you offer a fairly limited palette of choices, then your learners will learn how to make decisions and prove themselves trustworthy, while not being overwhelmed by the options. You can always increase the range of choice as your learners get more used to coping with this approach. You might offer your learners:

- a choice about which form or format to work in
- a choice about the order in which they complete a series of tasks
- a choice between two different sets of questions to answer
- a choice about which part of an activity to complete first
- a choice about who to work with in a group
- a choice about which role to take within a group
- a choice about whether to work alone or with others.

Techniques for effective group work

Working in a group can be tricky for learners, and it will not necessarily be trickiest for the learners that you might expect. Some learners who do absolutely fine when they are working individually can really struggle when you ask them to work in a group situation. Other learners only really get the chance to shine and to show what they can do when they are given the chance to work with a group of their peers. Before you set a group task it is useful to think about how different learners might react to it, and how you could adapt what you ask them to do to ensure that they all get the best out of the activity. Consider what each learner finds difficult, and how you could adapt the task to allow for this. Some of the difficulties that learners might encounter during group tasks include:

- waiting until it is their turn to participate without interrupting or trying to 'take over' the group
- taking other learners' ideas on board instead of wanting to have their own way all the time
- participating in any kind of group task
- not being drawn off task and into discussions that are not connected to the activity they are meant to be doing.

There are lots of ways in which to organise and differentiate group work to ensure that everyone participates and gets the best out of it. Think carefully about how you group your learners before you get started. Here are just a few ways to ensure that everyone contributes:

- Give out tokens such as raffle tickets, coins or poker chips, which your learners have to 'spend' when they make a contribution. Ask that everyone spends their tokens before the end of the allocated time.
- Give learners a different coloured pen each, and then ask them to write on a single sheet in those colours as they make their contributions. In this way, you can tell who has contributed what, which can feed into your assessment of the task.
- Allocate learners a role each, differentiating this according to the skills that they most need to develop, or the roles within which they work best.

Setting targets and timings

Setting targets and timings is a great way to encourage your learners to push themselves to reach for and surpass their limits. A target can motivate us to complete an activity and it can also cause us to think more deeply while doing an activity (for instance, if you ask your learners to summarise something in 'exactly 20 words'). Using targets and timings also allows you to differentiate according to your knowledge of an individual's needs. Perhaps you know that one learner needs pushing, and a sense of urgency, while another responds better to a more measured approach, and to being given plenty of time. Here are some ideas for utilising targets and timings in your classroom:

- In an ideas-gathering task, say to your learners: 'I want you to come up with at least ten, preferably 20, and quite possibly – if you are really pushing yourself – 30 ideas.'
- Tell your learners: 'When you have done x, then I want you to do y', or 'You can do x, once you have done y'.

- For a learner who struggles when given a lot of questions to complete at once, ask them to complete the even-numbered questions first, setting this as a doable target that they can reach and then beat.
- Give a particular learner more time to complete a task than their peers, if you know that they will need more time to think about their answers, or that they write more slowly than the others.
- Set a challenge for your high-attaining learners to produce more work in less time than their peers, or than an older year group.

Differentiating homework

As well as considering how to differentiate what goes on in your lessons, it is useful to think about differentiating your homework tasks as well. Remember that this doesn't necessarily mean setting different tasks for different learners – differentiation by task is time-consuming and it is often not the best available option. However, what this does mean is taking a long, hard look at whether all learners have the same chance to get some meaningful learning out of the tasks that you set for homework, or not – and, if the answer is 'no', reflecting on what that might realistically mean for how you approach the setting of them.

If we are completely honest with ourselves, homework can end up being more like busy work, rather than something for which a lot of forward thinking and planning goes into the process. Sometimes homework is a last-minute thought tacked on at the end of a lesson because we know we have to set it. It is important to ask ourselves whether it is really helpful for an individual to do five more examples of a sum that they have already done correctly 20 times in class. If the answer to the question is 'yes, to ensure they have grasped the skill', then all fine and good. However, if the answer is 'yes, because I have to set them something to do at home', then it may well be that there is a better alternative.

Ideally, to support differentiated learning, your homework should:

- **Have a clear purpose:** Preferably one that focuses on the understanding of a topic rather than just on repeating something that has already been understood.
- **Be simple enough to do:** Without requiring access to excessively complicated resources, particularly when you work with learners who might not have the support, the resources or the finances needed to do it at home. While that 'build a volcano' homework might seem fun from your perspective, from a parental viewpoint it may well not be.
- **Give the learners some sense of ownership:** To encourage them to learn more independently. You can achieve this by offering them some choices around how or what they do.

- **Be something that the learners can do without support, if they need to:** Support might not be on offer for every learner, and when we assess a homework in which parents or carers have made a substantial contribution, this can lead us to think that a learner can do something that they would not actually be able to do on their own.

When setting homework, think about whether all your learners will have the same chance to access it. If you are asking them to do something (e.g. cooking), do they all have the facilities or resources to do it? Do they have a quiet space in which to work? It is a good idea to let your learners have at least some ownership of their homework, at least some of the time, by making choices about what they do. This doesn't have to happen every time you set homework, but it is a handy way to ensure motivation and interest from your learners. The choices you give to your learners might include:

- **The form in which they present the homework:** For instance, as a booklet, a mind map, a 'lift the flaps', or a PowerPoint presentation. You could leave the choice entirely up to your learners, or you could give them a limited range of options.
- **The order in which they complete the tasks:** For instance, for a homework task that is set over several days or weeks.
- **The resources they use to complete the activity:** For example, handwritten or typed, or perhaps a choice of ebook versus textbook.

Consider giving a time limit for homework (e.g. 20 minutes of 'good old-fashioned hard work'), rather than making homework about completing x number of examples of something. You could ask parents to sign off to say their child has completed their 20 minutes of work, even if they didn't complete the task.

Flipped learning

The idea of flipped learning, or flipped homework, is a relatively new one, and it is essentially a logical response to the fact that we live in an age in which information is very freely available outside of school. If you haven't come across it before, the term 'flipped learning' simply means that you 'flip' the lesson, so that part of it happens before the lesson, rather than during class time or after it. This pre-learning could be about finding information, gathering knowledge, doing research or looking at articles or texts. The learning that has been done at home then feeds into the lesson that you do afterwards. With the explosion in the use of the Internet, our learners have access to more information than they can possibly know what to do with. Pointing this out, and reacting to it, is not the same thing as saying that learners don't need to memorise things in school anymore – clearly they still need to do this. However, instead of focusing on the negatives of online usage, it is surely a better idea to harness the power of the Internet to allow you to differentiate learning more effectively.

Remember that the 'flip' you offer doesn't have to be the same for everyone – flipping learning is a fairly straightforward way to differentiate by task. You might give your lower-attaining learners a text that you are going to refer to in class, or a list of key words for a new topic, which you feel they could do with reading beforehand. You could ask your highest-attaining learners to read a more complex article on a topic that you will study in class, or perhaps to prepare some materials for their peer group to read. You will need to account for the fact that some of your learners might not do the 'flip' that you have asked them to, and plan for this. Giving them a good reason to do the flipped learning is useful – for instance, telling them that they will have to share what they learnt with their peers.

Here are some suggestions for flipping the learning in your classroom:

- Create a video of some material that you will refer to in the next lesson, and ask your learners to watch it for homework.
- Give your learners a link to a YouTube video, or a documentary, that you want them to watch in preparation for what you will be doing in the next lesson.
- Share some articles that you would like the learners to read, and that you will refer to during class.
- Ask your learners to read a piece of text that you will be referring to in class, and stick sticky notes on it, to show the bits that they have questions about.
- Ask your learners to read a piece of text for the next lesson, and underline any words that they don't yet know.
- Ask your learners to find information, resources or materials to bring in and use in the next lesson.

It is all very well to say that we have taught something, but if the children haven't learned it, then we haven't really taught it. We need to consider how our teaching actually impacts on the children's learning. By reflecting on our own practice, we gain a clearer sense of how to better support understanding and we also build our skills in differentiating for the future.

Chapter 5
Assessment

Assessment is fundamental to differentiation, because unless we can figure out what a learner knows, understands or can do already, we will not be in a position to work out what they might need or want to learn next. An effective assessment will help us to work out where our learners are at the moment, and consequently it will give us information about where they need to go subsequently. As well as it being important for teachers to be aware of where their learners are at any given moment, it is also important for the learners themselves to understand where they are in their own learning. Teaching them how to assess their own strengths, weaknesses and gaps in understanding is incredibly helpful for their learning. This is commonly referred to as 'metacognition' – the process whereby we get our learners thinking about their own thinking.

It can be tempting to associate the word 'assessment' with tests and exams such as SATs and GCSEs, sat in silence then marked and graded. However, assessment comes in many different forms and formats. Assessment can be both formal and informal, and it happens all the time in a classroom. It is an ongoing process that plays a vital part in your everyday teaching. Assessment can of course take the form of the classic test – for instance, giving the learners a list of spellings to be memorised and then testing them on the spellings in class to see whether they have learnt them and remembered them accurately. Assessment can also be done via a series of multiple choice questions, designed to check for knowledge or understanding, at the start or end of a lesson. But assessment is also about the informal questions, observations, interviews and discussions with our learners that take place during lessons. Remember that assessment does not only have to be done *to* your learners, it can also be done *with* them as well.

The word 'assessment' comes originally from the Latin 'assidere', meaning to sit by. When we assess a learner, we metaphorically (or literally) sit beside them to discover what they have learnt. If we had the time and a ratio of one adult to one learner, we could talk with each learner one-to-one to find out more about what they have and haven't learnt. This is why personal tutoring can be so effective – because it is based on the reality in that moment of what an individual knows and can do, rather than on an estimate of where best to pitch a lesson for 30 different learners. If we were able to work one-to-one all the time, it would be much easier to base all future learning on exactly what each learner needs to do next. However, because we will often be working at a ratio of one to 30 learners (or more), a quick test in class is often the most practical way to assess their existing knowledge and understanding.

Differentiation is about a process of continuous decision-making, and assessment gives you information on which to base your decisions. How can you find out what this learner knows now? What should you do next to help this individual to learn? It is only when the teacher can look at evidence about how well the learners are progressing that we can decide what to do next, based on the evidence of progress (or the lack of it). Of course, it doesn't have to be the teacher who makes all the decisions – it is important to get the learners themselves and any support staff involved as well. The better the learners understand where they are, where they are going, and what they need to do next to get there, the better they will be able to learn.

Pre-assessment

Before you begin work on a unit or topic, you can use a pre-assessment to get a feel for where your learners are currently. A pre-assessment will help you find out what knowledge they have about a subject already, what misunderstandings or misconceptions they might have developed on a topic, and what they might still need or be interested in learning. What you discover might lead you to change your planning, or to adapt the lesson content for some groups or individuals who already know a lot about what you had planned to teach. Of course you might discover that the learners know *less* than you expected them to, as well as more. You could do your pre-assessment ahead of planning the unit of work, for instance fitting it in at the end of term, in preparation for a topic you will be covering at the start of the next one.

It is also possible to do some of these adaptations 'in the moment', for instance when you realise that a planned activity isn't working because your learners just don't have a grasp of an important prior concept. A good example of this is the time when I was on teaching practice and I tried to teach my Reception class group about the world, using a globe. I very quickly realised that they had no concept of 'the Earth' or of 'other countries', and that I needed to start with local geographical knowledge first.

Some useful pre-assessment questions would include:

- What do you think this topic is about?
- Can you give me some examples from or of this topic?
- What are the most important questions to ask here?

- What do you know about this already?
- What relevance might this topic have for you and your family?
- How could this topic link to your experiences in the wider world?
- Where do you think we will be going with this subject?
- What is there about this topic that really interests you?
- What other things would you like to know about this?

For older learners, a useful check for existing knowledge is to give them a list of the key words that they will encounter during the topic or area of study. You could then ask them to:

- write down a definition for as many of the words as they can
- write down anything else they know about any of the words (for instance, their etymology, any links to other subjects, etc.)
- explain how the key words are linked to each other in some way and show their reasoning
- create a diagram to show all the words that they already know that are linked to these key words
- write down any questions that they might want answered about any of these words.

As well as helping you to understand the learners' levels of pre-existing knowledge and/or skills, a pre-assessment can also help you find out about their level of interest in a topic. This is not to say that you should only teach your class about the things that they are already interested in, but that the information you glean could help you to think more fully about how to make the work feel more relevant and engaging to them. A single topic has the potential to be linked to lots of other areas and this is where your creative thinking as a teacher comes in handy.

Formative assessment

Formative assessment lets both the teacher and the learners know how well they are doing on an ongoing basis, as opposed to the kind of summative assessment that might happen at the end of a unit, a term or a year, and which is used to summarise progress over time. Formative assessment is about getting feedback to inform future learning, rather than being about giving grades that are recorded in a mark book. This kind of assessment is for both the learners and their teacher – it is part and parcel of a lesson, rather than a separate entity from it. Formative assessment is a great way to find out how well your teaching is working – if the learners don't 'get it' from the teaching you have done thus far, what might you need to adapt to ensure that they do?

Formative assessment should support the process of metacognition – it should encourage the learners to think about their own thinking and learning. It can be used to measure a variety of classroom outcomes: the knowledge gained, the skills developed and the understanding that has been achieved. The teacher uses formative assessment to identify what the learners can do well already, and so spot which parts of the learning process they still need to focus on. This in turn feeds into the decisions that the teacher uses to differentiate the learning. In order to be able to figure out what learning needs to come next, first we need to have a clear idea in our minds about what our end goal looks like. What are we actually aiming to get our learners to know, to understand and to be able to do?

Formative assessment can take a wide range of forms. The best form to use will depend on various factors, including the subject being studied and the age of the learners. Your formative assessment might be used to check for understanding, but you might also use it to check for misconceptions. Here are some of the techniques that you could use:

- an oral conference with an individual or a small group
- a series of written responses
- a checklist to identify which skills each learner has mastered
- a whole-class response to a series of questions (this could be verbal or visual, e.g. 'hands up if you…')
- an interview with a learner
- a mind map or concept map of the topic being studied, either drawn by individuals or completed in groups
- a computer survey (for instance using **surveymonkey.com**)
- a graphic where the learners show what has been learnt
- a series of questions that are asked and answered by individuals
- a task completed on mini whiteboards, which are held up to show the teacher
- a short written summary of what they have learnt, for instance in a single sentence or in 20 words
- a 'show me five' query, where learners hold up a number of fingers between one and five, depending on whether they're unsure about a topic (one finger) or totally confident (five fingers)
- an 'exit card', where you ask a question about the topic and the learners leave their answers on a small piece of paper to show whether they've really understood the lesson content.

Summative assessment

Summative assessment comes at the end of a period of learning – it 'sums up' what has been learnt (or at least what we hope has been learnt). Summative assessment might take the form of an end-of-topic test, end-of-year exams, or more formal tests such as SATs and GCSEs. Although it's not a method that is very widely used in school classrooms, summative assessment could also potentially take the form of a portfolio or a body of work collected over time. It could summarise an individual's learning in the sense of giving examples of the best pieces that they have done during a period in their education.

When we are considering how best to differentiate, summative assessment is important because:

- **It helps us to track each learner's progress over time:** Are they keeping up momentum, moving ahead or perhaps falling backwards in their learning compared to the rest of the cohort? If an individual is out of line with where you think they should be, this might lead you to consider how much effort they are putting in, but also how well you are differentiating for them. What adaptations or supports might you need to put in place to get them back on track?
- **It helps us to check how well we taught a particular part of the curriculum, or even a single item within a wider topic area:** If all your learners do badly on one specific aspect of a summative assessment, you would need to ask yourself questions about the way you taught that particular area. Did you cover it in sufficient detail? Was there a problem with the way that you explained it? Were some of the learners absent from class when you covered this area? If it is clear that there is a gap in the learning, you would need to make plans to revisit it with all or some of your learners.
- **It can help us to identify those individual learners who have problems with particular areas of the curriculum, and consequently to put support in place to differentiate for them:** Where we can highlight an issue with a specific skill, this might support us in identifying a special educational need, such as dyslexia.
- **It encourages learners to go back over their learning:** They revisit and revise it and see where any gaps might be in preparation for and in response to a test. It can be used to promote and encourage independent study.
- **It can act as a motivator for learners to study:** However, we also need to accept that summative tests can be demotivating for those learners who do not 'pass' or meet 'expected standards'. The idea that ranking learners will encourage them to work harder is often a case of wishful thinking.

Creating effective assessments

Creating effective assessments is not easy – there are entire organisations dedicated to designing the tests and exams that are set in schools, to ensure that they are fair, accurate and that they test the things they are meant to be testing. Even then, we still regularly see mistakes being made by testing organisations. When we create and use assessments in the classroom with our learners, we need to be clear in our minds about what purpose that assessment will serve – what are we trying to find out and why are we looking to discover it? What impact will it have on the differentiation that we do in our classrooms?

The starting point for answering these questions will lie in the timing of the test.

- Is it a pre-assessment, designed to find out what the learners already know, so that we can differentiate for them during a topic or a series of lessons?
- Is it a formative assessment, created to discover how well the teaching is working as you go along, so that you know whether you are meeting every learner's needs?
- Or is it a summative assessment, intended to summarise a period of learning that has already taken place, to find out how well each of your learners has understood or retained what was being studied?

When creating an assessment, it is vital to define your learning objectives – what kind of things do you/did you intend the learners to learn and how can you find out whether all or some of them already know them, or whether they have learnt them from being in your lessons? It sounds obvious to say, but if the test is at the end of a unit, and is designed to see how well the learners have understood or retained what you taught, you should make sure that you base it on the things that were actually in your lessons.

The form that the assessment takes will vary according to your objectives for the test. If you want to find out whether your learners can write an explanation, a set of multiple choice questions will not be particularly helpful. If you want to know whether the learners have remembered the facts that you taught them, a quiz might be your best bet. If you want to test their speaking and/or listening skills, you are going to have to do an oral assessment. When it comes to assessment, we need to choose the right tool for the job – you don't use a hammer to insert a screw. It can be useful to think about assessments in terms of key knowledge, understanding and skills:

- What facts, definitions and vocabulary do I want to find out if the learners know?

- What principles, concepts and ideas do I want to find out if the learners understand?
- What processes and skills do I want to see if the learners can demonstrate?

You might also want to think about the personal attributes and attitudes that you want your learners to develop, although these aspects can be much trickier to test using an in-class assessment, since they are by definition nebulous. There are some specifically-designed assessments based around the idea of how engaged, focused, etc. your learners are – for instance, the Leuven Wellbeing Scales that are sometimes used in early years settings. When you are testing for progress in these kinds of areas, a checklist can be a useful format to use, because it highlights what your learners 'can do'.

When you are thinking about creating assessments, it is helpful to consider the following questions:

- Which bit of knowledge, skill or understanding do I plan to test for – what is the specific learning objective I am testing them on?
- Am I checking to see if a target was achieved? How will I define the target?
- What skills or concepts am I assuming the learners have already?
- What am I going to do with the information I get from this assessment?
- How will I use this information to move everyone forwards?
- How will I use this information to move individual learners forwards?
- What is the main or overarching purpose of the assessment?
- How am I going to track progress over time – what method of data collection will I use?
- What impact might doing this assessment have on individual motivation, particularly for any learners who find it impossible to access?
- How can I make this assessment hard enough to check the point that the higher-attaining learners have reached, while still ensuring that it is accessible for those who struggle?

Bear in mind that any written assessment will be testing your learners' knowledge of English, as much as it is testing their knowledge of a subject or an area of skill. If you are working with a class that has lots of learners with EAL, or if you work with learners who have specific types of SEND, then you may well need to differentiate the tests you set, or give additional support to specific learners so that they are able to access them. For instance, you might do this by reading the questions out loud to some learners, or by offering a translated text. Make sure that you are actually testing for the thing you think you are testing for. It could be that you need to offer some of your learners the chance to opt out of an assessment, or to complete it with individual support, especially a test that is going to be inaccessible for them.

Finding assessments

There is no point in replicating work that has already been done. It may well be that you can find a suitable assessment for your learners without needing to design your own, or that you can adapt something that someone else has already made. Some of the places where you might source assessments that have already been created include:

- in a textbook that you have been using with the learners in class, or one that covers the area you have been studying in a similar way to your lesson plans
- via other members of your department in a secondary school
- from a fellow class teacher within the same year group in a primary school
- online (although make sure that you source these from reputable organisations and check them for content before using them with your learners)
- past papers from exams such as SATs or GCSEs.

Designing assessments

There will be times when you feel that your best bet is to create an assessment of your own. Perhaps you want to test for something specific, and you can't find a template that matches it. Maybe the range of attainment in your class is too wide for a pre-made assessment to work. When you design your own assessments, remember to:

- **Ensure that the instructions are clear and unambiguous:** Just as giving instructions in class is a bit of an art form, so too is writing clear test instructions.
- **Be very clear about the timing of the test:** How long will the learners have to complete the test as a whole, and what might this indicate for how long they should spend on each answer? Think carefully about how long you should allow – it can be tricky to strike a balance between some learners finishing very early and others having enough time to complete it. It is worth considering whether, if the test is easy enough for some learners to finish it early, you are really testing for the same thing when other learners need lots of extra time on top.
- **Make sure that the wording of questions is clear and simple:** Don't allow any ambiguity to creep into the way that you phrase things. For instance,

ensure that you steer clear of idiomatic language that might confuse learners who have EAL.

- **Consider setting easier questions at the start of the test, and gradually increasing the difficulty:** This will help ensure that all your learners set off on a positive track.
- **Think ahead about scoring and what form this will take:** Will it be marks, percentages, grades or a mixture? Are you going to give partial credit to learners who get an answer partly right? Are you going to give credit for showing working out?
- **Consider asking a colleague to check it over for you:** Whenever you design an assessment, it is worth getting a colleague to check it over for you. They might well spot issues, confusions or pitfalls that you hadn't noticed.

If your assessment is designed to be objective (i.e. to lead to a yes/no answer, rather than a more subjective response), then the following tips should help you design an effective assessment:

- **Ensure that the area being tested actually *is* objective:** Are you 100 per cent sure that what you are asking is not subjective and based on opinion? For instance, in a subject such as grammar, definitive answers can be tricky, because grammar changes over time, and because it is partly about interpretation.
- **Phrase your questions so that there actually is only one best and 'correct' answer:** This can be surprisingly hard to do.
- **Make sure that you randomise the position of the correct answer each time:** For instance, varying whether it falls as A, B, C or D on alternate questions.
- **Phrase your questions in a positive way:** For clarity of communication, phrase your questions in a positive way, rather than using negatives, such as 'which one is not an example of x'.

Linking assessments to learning

When you give a class assessment, make sure that you explain to your learners *why* they are doing it – what is its purpose, what information are you trying to find out, and how will it help them and feed into their learning in the future? When you explain to your learners why they are being tested, this helps them to see the value of the test and to understand its potential impact on them. One of the reasons why the end of key stage tests (SATs) in England can be so stressful and annoying for learners is because the answer to the question 'Why are we doing this test?' is 'To measure your school'. It must be hard for any learner to see a valid purpose in that, beyond a concern that they don't let their school or teacher down by doing badly.

Your answer to the question 'Why are we doing this assessment?' will help you ensure that your assessments relate closely to your learning objectives. You can also stress how the assessments you do inform you when it comes to differentiating to meet everyone's needs. For instance, you might say:

- 'We are doing this test to check which of these spellings you already know/ have retained, and which of them I still need to help you learn.'
- 'We are doing this test to find out whether you've all understood this part of the topic in the way I taught it, and whether we are ready to move onto the next bit.'
- 'We are doing this assessment to discover what you already know about this topic, so I don't accidentally teach it to you twice.'
- 'We are doing this assessment to find out what you remember from studying this subject last year, and which bits of the subject I need to go over again.'
- And, perhaps, 'We are doing this assessment to see which ones of you did your homework or studied for this test.'

Involving the learners in assessment

To be fully effective, assessment needs to do more than just give teachers information about how their learners are progressing and how well their approaches are working. An effective assessment should also help the learners themselves understand more about where they are in their learning, about how they operate as learners, and about what targets they might be aiming to achieve next. It should involve an element of self-reflection and self-evaluation. By involving the learners in judgements about their own learning, you help them to develop the skill of metacognition – to think about their own thinking.

Some of your learners may have a negative view of assessment: perhaps they associate it more with tests and pressure, rather than with learning being differentiated to meet their needs. Perhaps they have failed in many of the tests they have taken previously, and this has left them disaffected with the idea of being measured. With so many high-stakes tests now punctuating a child's primary school career in England, it is perhaps easy to see why some learners might feel this way. Assessment has come to feel like something that is done to them, rather than done with them. The teacher administers the tests, the teacher or an external body marks the tests, and the results are compared to other learners across the country. The learners are then ranked according to where they sit on a national scale.

Ideally, we want the learners to understand both the process of assessment, and also how it can inform and support them in their personal education. We want them to be able to work out where they are now and be able to set themselves targets to work towards. We want them to become more aware of the kinds of approaches that work for them when it comes to learning effectively and efficiently. This will set them up well for independent study and build their confidence around learning. This is not the same thing as learners being able to parrot a target or a target grade for an inspector; it needs to be about developing a genuine understanding of their own learning and their own learning needs.

To involve your learners in assessing their own learning, you might ask them to:

- **Give immediate feedback on their understanding of a key idea or how well they feel they have grasped a key skill:** For instance, by holding up a red, orange or green card to signal their level of confidence.
- **Show a quick thumbs up or thumbs down:** To indicate whether they understand and you are okay to proceed, or whether you need to explain something over again.
- **Grade their own work when they have finished, for attainment and/or effort:** Encourage them to be honest about how much effort they really put in.
- **Assess and critique other learners' work:** This can be either individually or as a group.
- **Complete a quick quiz on a topic:** Not as a formal assessment but to check their own understanding.
- **Talk about their feelings around learning, and about their motivation levels:** Ask them to identify what they need to help them feel positive and motivated.
- **Identify specific strategies for learning:** For instance, creating mnemonics, and asking them to assess how confident they would feel about doing this independently.
- **Create their own mark schemes:** Using their own work as an example and creating a rubric that shows what they are looking for in a 'good' piece of work.

Assessment and unlearning

You might have noticed how it is often the case that, despite being taught something and apparently having understood it fully in a lesson, some learners will still fail to show that they have learnt it next time around. For some reason, the learning is not yet secure or it has not stuck. For example, despite years of practice in using punctuation correctly, some learners still carry on not putting any full stops in their work. Or even after years of practising and being tested on multiplication tables, some learners still cannot remember 7 x 8. What is going on for these learners, and how can we differentiate for them?

When you come across a learner who appears to have unlearnt or forgotten something, it is important to think carefully about the reasons why this might be. It could be the case that:

- The learner did once remember what you taught them, but has now forgotten it, perhaps due to not using it in a while.
- The learner didn't retain the concept, skill or information beyond the initial lesson in which it was taught.
- The learner did not understand the concept, skill or information in the first place, and perhaps you didn't notice their lack of understanding in the lesson.
- The learner couldn't find a way to make the information stick in their mind (7 x 8 is known to be one of the trickiest of the times tables to retain). Perhaps it just wasn't memorable enough when they originally learnt it.
- The learner has an issue with short- or long-term memory – they have a problem with the cognitive processes required to make something stick.
- The learner is not sufficiently motivated to do or remember this particular thing, even though in theory they know how to do it correctly. This often seems to be the case with errors in skills such as punctuation.

To differentiate for those learners who seem to 'unlearn' the things you teach them, you could:

- Set a separate homework, based on revising an area that is secure for the rest of your class but is not secure for this learner.
- Offer them specific memory techniques and strategies. For example, to remember 7 x 8 = 56, it can be useful to think of the numerical sequence: 5, 6, 7, 8.
- Help them learn how to visualise information – some learners don't understand that it is possible to make 'mental pictures' to help them understand or retain concepts.
- Get the learner to focus on the small things for a while, until they are truly retained – for instance, setting a target to focus only on ensuring that there are always full stops in their writing before trying to introduce other forms of punctuation.
- Create a motivator for 'getting it right'. For instance, making a positive phone call home after a week in which the learner's writing always includes full stops.

- Talk to the learner to examine and analyse the reasons *why* they struggle to retain this particular piece of information or skill. For instance, in the case of full stops, does the learner actually understand how a sentence is constructed and what it must contain?

Spaced learning

The idea of 'spaced learning' has come to prominence in recent years, particularly when dealing with memorising factual information. The idea is that you teach something multiple times, but over an extended period. Between each time of teaching, you allow the learners a period of time to 'forget' the information, before teaching it to them again. It is believed that this might help the information stick in your learners' long-term memory.

Informal assessments

Teachers spend their working lives in a heightened state of awareness about how their learners are doing – both in terms of their academic progress and also in the sense of their self-confidence, mood, behaviour, motivation and so on, which all feed into their making progress in learning (or not). When you are doing these informal assessments, you might not even be aware that you are doing them, because they happen subconsciously and intuitively, particularly as you gain in experience. You gather a 'sense' of where the learners are at any particular moment, which can feed into your planning for each individual – this is all part of what good teaching involves. You might be hard put to write down specific information that you gain from these informal moments in your classroom, but they are likely to play a key part in your thinking on differentiation. The more you can notice and articulate them, the better placed you will be to explain what 'differentiation' looks like in your classroom.

Below you can find some examples of the kind of informal assessments that teachers do on a daily basis and how this might feed into their teaching and their thinking about how to differentiate.

- **You watch the learners as they enter the room, to get a sense for what kind of mood the group is in:** Perhaps you notice that they seem very excitable so you throw in an activity to calm them down, before you begin your lesson. Or maybe you see that they look lethargic and sluggish so you do a short physical warm-up to get them alert.
- **You observe the learners as they leave the room, to get a 'feel' for how they reacted to your lesson:** You notice a 'buzz' of energy and reflect on which

of the strategies you used might have created this. Or, you notice that the learners look tired and disinterested, and you think about how you could teach the same topic in a more engaging way.

- **You stand back and listen in on your learners' discussions when they are working in a group:** You notice that one learner is very reticent to get involved in the conversation. You consider the strategies that you could use to boost this learner's confidence and to encourage participation from all group members.
- **You look to see what a learner's facial expressions, posture or gestures can tell you about how they are feeling or reacting:** You notice an individual biting their nails and you ask gently about whether anything is troubling them. You spot that an individual looks really excited on a Monday morning and you ask them if they want to share any good news with the class.

Observations, assessment and learning

Something that we rarely have time to do in our classrooms is to take the time to simply stand back and observe what our learners are doing, but we should bear in mind that this certainly qualifies as an form of assessment. In an early years setting, there are often a reasonable number of chances to stand back and observe the children at work and play, because observational assessments are seen as a key part of good practice. However, as our learners get older we tend to feel that we must be constantly teaching them or working with them. It seems almost sacrilege to suggest that we could stand back and take some time to watch our learners at work on their learning. How could they possibly be learning if we are not busy teaching them, intervening in their learning and going through activities with them? What if someone was to look in your classroom and catch you simply observing, rather than doing?

The problem, though, is that a lack of time spent observing learning can lead to misunderstandings and problematic assumptions. It can lead to us rushing in to intervene, rather than standing back to figure out what is really going on. It is all too easy to get so focused on the small details that we can miss the bigger picture. A great example of this is with group work. The moment the teacher moves in to 'work with' a group, the group dynamic shifts. Exactly the same thing can happen when you intervene in children's play. The learners will often start to do or say what they think you want them to, rather than carrying on doing what they were doing before you got involved. Sometimes this can be a good thing – for instance, where you need to guide a group back on task or move their discussion in a specific direction – but sometimes it can just 'freeze them up'.

While you might be observing what your learners know and can do, it is often the case that an observation will highlight a particular aspect of a learner's personality or an attitude to learning. In turn, this can help you figure out how you could differentiate for them in the future, or how you might need to adapt the task the next time you set something similar. For instance, in a group task, you might observe that:

- one learner takes over and immediately starts issuing commands and doing all the talking
- another learner sits back and lets the others run the group
- one learner speaks out confidently while another mumbles their ideas and gets talked over
- another learner gazes off into space and refuses to get involved
- another learner spends most of the time fiddling with the resources rather than concentrating on what is going on.

To overcome these issues, you might use some of the techniques and strategies for effective group work described in Chapter 4 (page 98–9).

Observations and the teaching space

Another useful thing about sitting or stepping back and doing an observation is that it can give you a sense of how the learners operate within the classroom, which in turn can lead to interesting conclusions about how well your teaching space is organised and how this might or might not support differentiated learning. Making observations in this way can give you some interesting and even startling insights into how individuals learn. In the same way that a business might do a 'time and motion study' to come to conclusions about efficient practices in a workplace, so you can do a study to see how the learners use your classroom space as well. You can learn a lot by doing this yourself, but you might also encourage your learners to make observations about their behaviours within the space too.

As well as observing your learners' behaviour in and movements around the space, you can also track them by drawing them as a diagram. Where did they go and how long did they spend in each place? This is particularly fascinating to do in a free-flow environment such as an early years setting. From your observations, you might notice that:

- some spaces in your room get much more use than others
- some areas get barely any use at all
- learners tend to 'cluster' in specific parts of the room
- there are obstacles to movement that you hadn't really considered before
- accessing resources has the potential to lead to conflict because of the way that the space is set out
- it is often the unplanned interactions between learners that lead either to great learning or to unfortunate conflicts.

Marking and feedback

Marking, and its close relative feedback, are subjects that are widely discussed, and on which there are probably as many different opinions as there are teachers. In recent years, excessively prescriptive marking policies led to a significant increase in teacher workload, unacceptably so in some schools. The need to have 'evidence of progress' has resulted in teachers being asked to evidence progress through writing comments and targets in their learners' books. Thankfully Ofsted and the DfE are finally taking steps to address this issue by making it clear that there is no 'expected' way in which teachers should mark. In reality though, marking has always been and continues to be part of the job of being a teacher. By noticing errors, praising positives and offering ideas for improvement, we can help learners improve their learning.

Marking has many benefits in terms of getting to know your learners, and therefore in being able to differentiate more effectively for them:

- **Marking allows you to assess how well individual children have understood something taught in class:** For instance, when you mark some sums that they did independently in a maths class.
- **When you mark, this encourages (or even forces) you to look through the work that your learners did in class:** The marking you do doesn't have to be detailed for you to gain a sense of where the learners are; you can get a feel for this from just looking through their books.
- **You can identify specific areas of need or next steps for individuals:** By looking through your learners' written work.
- **Written feedback can be a very useful motivator:** Seeing an adult 'make marks' on their work is a great way to praise and encourage your learners.
- **Your marking can inform future learning:** Your learners can look back at the work that was done previously, and the corrections you made to it or the comments you made on it, and use this to inform their future learning.
- **By giving some kind of grade, for either effort or attainment or both, you give the learners a sense of how well they are doing in their work:** You also gain evidence that will show you progress made (or not) over time.
- **You and the learners can set targets as part of the marking and feedback process:** This will, in turn, help them think in more detail about where they are with their learning and where they need to go next.

Marking offers a great way to differentiate, because you don't have to mark in exactly the same way, or for exactly the same thing, for every learner. If you were planning to mark each book anyway, you can personalise the way that you mark to individual needs, without adding to your workload at all. For instance, you could:

- **Set individual learners specific targets:** You can set these in class, and let them know that you will be marking specifically to check whether they have aimed for and met them.
- **Mark for specific errors:** You can check that one learner uses full stops correctly, while another remembers to split their writing into paragraphs.
- **Set activities in response to marking:** For instance, writing out spellings three times in the back of their books so that feedback is personalised to individual weaknesses and needs.

You can also involve your learners in the marking process, and get them to think about how feedback improves their performance. You might:

- **Ask the learners to identify what aspect of their writing they would like you to mark:** This will help them learn how to think about and set their own targets for improvement.
- **Give a code instead of a comment:** The code relates to the target for the individual. In class, you can then explain how the codes link to comments, and your learners can write out the comments in their books as their next targets.
- **Discuss the learning that has been done in groups:** Getting your learners to look at, assess, critique and mark each other's work.

Remember that feedback doesn't have to be written – verbal feedback is also a highly valuable part of your practice, and one that often happens naturally during lessons. When thinking about how to differentiate verbal feedback, consider whether a learner will respond best to a critique, or whether you are better to focus on praising what has been done well to boost their confidence.

Using technology for assessment

More and more, technology offers a great way to support differentiation for your learners. One key way that technology can support you is in the way that it makes it very easy to embed a quick assessment into your lesson. For instance, after doing a short period of direct teaching about a new topic, you could give your learners a set of five questions on what you have just taught them. Using an app such as *Nearpod* (**nearpod.com**) or similar, the learners answer the questions on a mobile device, and you can see what progress they have made and where there are errors or misconceptions.

Other ways in which technology can help you with differentiated assessment could include the use of video or recorded feedback. Not only can this be quicker and more informative than marking a book, but learners can also listen to it as many times as they like, to understand your comments. They might also usefully refer back to it when doing a similar piece of work in the future.

Ofsted

While we should never differentiate *for* Ofsted, it is certainly the case that inspectors would wish to see us making maximum progress for each learner, through the use of both support and challenge. Knowing why and how to differentiate is one of the most effective ways we can possibly do this, because we are focusing on the learning of each individual. In addition, it's important to remember that the requirement to differentiate is in the *Teachers' Standards* (DfE, 2011), and it is therefore the case that it is a statutory minimum duty for schools.

In preparation for Ofsted, and during an inspection:

- **Be confident about the myriad of ways in which you differentiate:** Refuse to get trapped into thinking that the only kind of differentiation that matters is the kind that you can note down on a piece of paper.
- **Where you are using subtle and perhaps not easily spotted methods, make these explicit for a visiting inspector:** Do this by talking about them with the inspector in a feedback session, if you possibly can.
- **Demonstrate how you have reflected on and adapted your practice in order to ensure that you meet the needs of individual learners:** For instance, by showing how you have linked your planning to the marking you have done, e.g. that you have identified that several learners have an issue with a particular skill, and adapted your next lesson to reflect this.

Conclusion

As I noted at the start of this book, so much of the differentiation you do is about the subtle adaptations you make in your classroom, as a result of your knowledge of each young person you are teaching. When we understand what individual learners know and can do, and how they might build on their learning, we put ourselves in the best possible position to support and challenge them. When we learn to reflect on our own practice, and use a range of resources, strategies and approaches to help our learners understand the learning, we can get as close as possible to personalising the learning journey for each child.

I hope that this book will help you feel confident in your professional judgement and consequently able to say to anyone who visits your classroom: this is what differentiation means to me.

Bibliography

DfE (2011), *Teachers' Standards*. Crown copyright

Drabble, C. (2016), *Bloomsbury CPD Library: Supporting Children with Special Educational Needs and Disabilities*. London: Bloomsbury

Early Education (2012), *Development Matters in the Early Years Foundation Stage (EYFS)*. London: Early Education (www.foundationyears.org.uk/files/2012/03/Development-Matters-FINAL-PRINT-AMENDED.pdf)

Gedge, N. (2016), *Inclusion for Primary School Teachers*. London: Bloomsbury

QCA (2000), *Curriculum Guidance for the Foundation Stage*. London: Qualifications and Curriculum Authority

Index

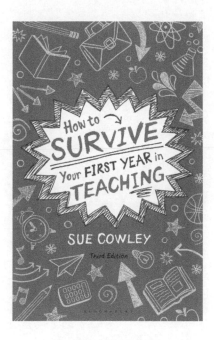

Also available from Sue Cowley